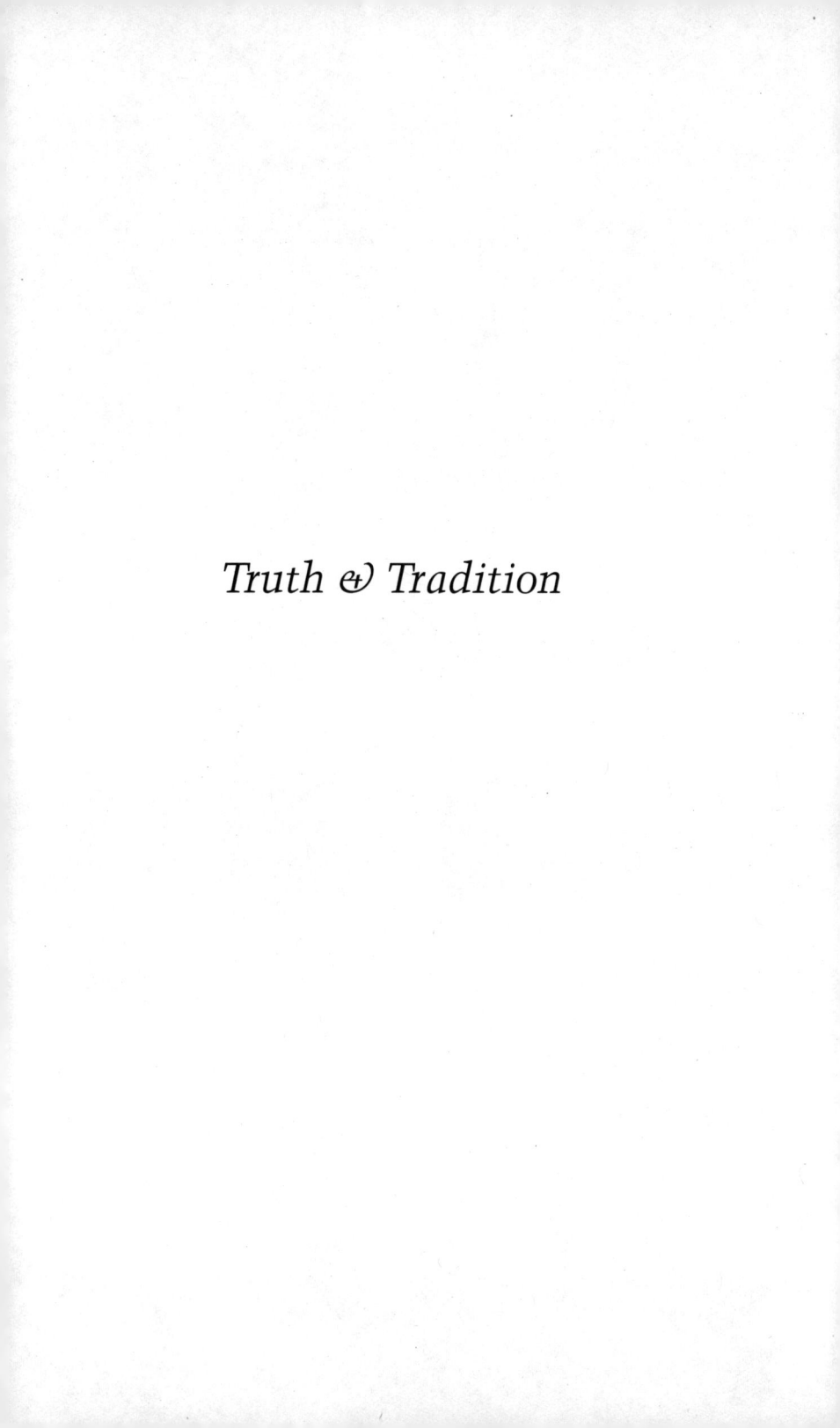

Truth & Tradition

Truth & Tradition

A Conversation About the Future of United Methodist Theological Education

EDITED BY
Neal F. Fisher

ABINGDON PRESS
NASHVILLE

TRUTH AND TRADITION

Copyright © 1995 by Abingdon Press

All rights reserved.
No part of this work may be reproduced or transmitted in any form or by any means, electronic or mechanical, including photocopying and recording, or by any information storage or retrieval system, except as may be expressly permitted by the 1976 Copyright Act or in writing from the publisher. Requests for permission should be addressed to Abingdon Press, P.O. Box 801, 201 Eighth Avenue South, Nashville TN 37202.

This book is printed on recycled, acid-free paper.

Library of Congress Cataloging-in-Publication Data

Truth & tradition: a conversation about the Future of United
Methodist theological education/edited by Neal F. Fisher.
    p.   cm.
  Includes index.
  ISBN 0-687-00810-7 (alk. paper)
    1. Theology—Study and teaching—United Methodist Church (U.S.)
2. Theology—Study and teaching—United States. 3. Methodist theological seminaries—United States. 4. United Methodist Church (U.S.)—Education. 5. Methodist Church—United States—Education.
I. Fisher, Neal F. (Neal Floyd), 1936– . II. Title: Truth and tradition.
BX8219.T78   1995
207'.1'176—dc20   95-5894
                                                                                                               CIP

Scripture quotations, unless otherwise indicated, are from the New Revised Standard Version Bible, copyright © 1989 by the Division of Christian Education of the National Council of the Churches of Christ in the United States of America.

Scripture quotations noted NEB are from *The New English Bible*. © The Delegates of the Oxford University Press and The Syndics of the Cambridge University Press 1961, 1970. Reprinted by permission.

The excerpt from *The Book of Discipline* on page 59 is from *The Book of Discipline of the United Methodist Church—1992*. Copyright © 1992 by The United Methodist Publishing House. Used by Permission.

95 96 97 98 99 00 01 02 03 04—10 9 8 7 6 5 4 3 2 1

MANUFACTURED IN THE UNITED STATES OF AMERICA

IN MEMORY:
Floyd R. Fisher
Florence A. Fisher
First theological teachers
—N.F.F.

Contents

Foreword	Roger W. Ireson	9
Chapter 1	Context and Concern *Neal F. Fisher*	13
Chapter 2	Truth and Tradition *Robert C. Neville*	37
Chapter 3	Leaders and Servants *Lovett H. Weems, Jr.*	59
Chapter 4	Freedom and Accountability *Judith E. Smith*	76
Chapter 5	Congregation and Academy *Anne Streaty Wimberly and Edward P. Wimberly*	93
Chapter 6	Immigrants and Pioneers *Neal F. Fisher*	111
Contributors		136
Seminaries of The United Methodist Church		138
Index		139

Foreword

To find the origin of the relationship between the church and academia, one must go back through the mists of time to the academy in Athens and the rabbis' teaching steps excavated in recent years at the entrance of the temple mount in Jerusalem. The latter site is especially important for expressing the purpose of seminaries in the life of the church, because it reminds us of the teaching that Jesus rendered to the disciples and seekers during his ministry in Jerusalem. This same teaching tradition is perpetuated in the life of the seminary of our day. Our tradition is grounded in the noble search for truth and ultimate meaning which so characterized intellectual inquiry among the Greeks and was introduced into church life through the writings of Paul. Yet at the same time, our tradition is also rooted in the fervent search for divine presence revealed in justice, mercy, and grace as realized through community in the Hebrew legacy. The ultimate expression of this mission is found in the life and teachings of the master teacher, Jesus of Nazareth. Thus the church has borne the tradition of reason and faith through the ages, per-

Foreword

petuating a Greek and a Hebrew legacy of learning, albeit expressed in variant forms in different periods.

One recalls the great thinkers of the Christian tradition to find expressed in every age the important relationship of faith and intellect. Augustine, Anselm, Thomas Aquinas, Gabriel Biel, Martin Luther, Jr., John Calvin, John Wesley, John Henry Newman, Karl Barth, Paul Tillich, Gerhard Ebeling, Hans Küng, Martin Luther King, Jr., Karl Rahner, and a host of others could be summoned to show the relationship between faith and the intellectual life in the church. Through periods of profound change, the centers of intellectual life in the church have provided theological reflection and insight which have guided the church in its ministry. In each age, the church has sought through its seminary communities the means to express the faith in fresh and engaging forms to win a new generation to Christian belief and life.

We have entered another turbulent time in the life of the church and its seminaries. A pluralistic society with new understandings and insights has challenged the educational process itself. The questions that have been raised seek to establish a broader understanding of content as well as method. The movement to a new century carries within it disturbing queries concerning what is most needed for ministry in a new era of rapid change experienced in technological transformation and a multicultural, multiracial society. As one moves from conference to conference, the questions often raised concern the seminaries and ministerial education. A plethora of opinions is offered. One such assertion suggested that the entire seminary curriculum should be built around ministry in a drug culture. A week later another person suggested that most churches are small and in rural settings so that these factors must dominate seminary preparation. Still another voice asserted in a subsequent conference that seminarians should learn more administration and

Foreword

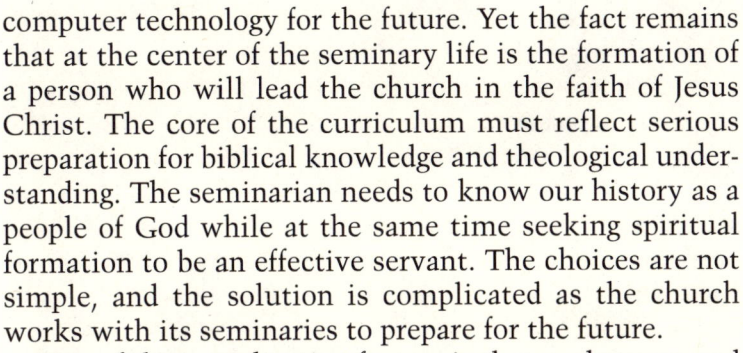

computer technology for the future. Yet the fact remains that at the center of the seminary life is the formation of a person who will lead the church in the faith of Jesus Christ. The core of the curriculum must reflect serious preparation for biblical knowledge and theological understanding. The seminarian needs to know our history as a people of God while at the same time seeking spiritual formation to be an effective servant. The choices are not simple, and the solution is complicated as the church works with its seminaries to prepare for the future.

One of the complicating factors is that we have moved a significant distance from the time when theological studies were conducted in the fellowship of small communities with an uncomplicated curriculum and a final examination by the bishop or the bishop's representative. The modern theological seminary, while related to the church through history and commitment, nonetheless does not receive funding from the church in the same measure as it once did. Today, our seminaries receive less than 20 percent of their support directly from the church and depend upon students to make up the difference in tuition payments. Many of these students are from different denominations from the church that founded the seminary. At the same time, the costs of administering an educational institution have risen, as has student indebtedness. Most students make their choice of seminary on the basis of financial aid. While committed to ecumenism, there is a growing awareness that educational formation in a denominational seminary creates a greater awareness of the life and ethos of the denomination while preparing future ministers for more effective ministry by linking the seminary with the local church.

Through all of this transition in our culture and times, The United Methodist Church has maintained thirteen of the finest seminaries in the United States and many similar institutions in the world. The quality of leadership

Foreword

from our deans and presidents, along with the superb scholarship and faith commitment of our faculties, has meant that a new generation of seminarians is being prepared to assume a leadership role in the life of the church during one of the most challenging times of history. Recently the seminaries in the United States have sought to be in dialogue with the church. The results have been impressive both in terms of insight gained and affirmation received in regard to the fine educational work being carried on in the midst of the confusing and difficult emerging contexts of our day. The task of theological education is a collegial calling to which we must all make our commitment in the church.

In this book, one will find the reflection and insight that will help us all to prepare for the future while fulfilling the great intellectual and spiritual heritage we have received. We commend this book to you for your careful study as another important resource in the continuing discussion about preparation for the sacred task of ministry in the modern world.

Roger W. Ireson, Ph.D.
General Secretary
General Board of Higher Education and Ministry
The United Methodist Church

Chapter One

Context and Concern

Neal F. Fisher

The purpose of this book is to help inform a continuing conversation in the church concerning the future of United Methodist theological education. This conversation is encouraged in the conviction that, humanly speaking, nothing is more central for the future of the church than committed, visionary, capable leadership. Most of us embraced faith in Christ because of someone who was herself or himself a disciple. Some parent, teacher, pastor, friend, or spouse communicated the meaning of the biblical faith in a winning way, and we were led either to affirm the faith in which we were reared or to embrace it for the first time.

We do not know all the designs of God for the denomination of which we are a part, but we may be assured that the church cannot be the faithful body it needs to be without leadership that is called and prepared. Theological education is devoted to preparing effective leaders, bold visionaries who will discern the divine stirrings in our midst and draw upon the gifts given to the community to worship God and serve in Christ's name.

The United Methodist Church approaches the discussion of theological education in a distinctive manner. Our movement was born on a university campus, Oxford University, and it has consistently stressed the importance of

Truth and Tradition

loving God with one's mind. Predecessors to this denomination also grew as part of a revival movement in England and the United States, licked by the flames of the Spirit and devoted at the outset primarily to common people who were not the products of the universities. Genetically we are predisposed to some ambivalence about theological education. There are "family resemblances," as we shall see, between the debates over the seminaries in the 1850s and some present discussions nearly a century and a half later. It is well, therefore, for us to begin the conversation by noting the context in which it takes place and the concerns that have characterized United Methodists and our predecessors throughout the lifetime of this movement.

RECOGNIZING THE NEED

There were important ventures in formal theological education in the United States before the predecessors of United Methodism were a force in the new nation. The Great Awakening that swept through the colonies in the late 1730s and 1740s challenged traditional patterns of the churches. The Presbyterians were split between those who favored the revivals and those who opposed them. During the Great Awakening, Gilbert Tennent preached his famous sermon "The Danger of an Unconverted Clergy" (1740), in which he concluded that the academies were corrupted and that the church therefore should establish "private schools, or seminaries of learning, which are under the care of skillful and experienced Christians" to prepare a more faithful converted clergy.[1] This and other similar sentiments led the Presbyterians to establish educational institutions and apprenticeship programs to prepare a clergy with pro-revival sentiments.

Context and Concern

In the 1790s, the heirs of the first Great Awakening experienced a resurgence of revivals and religious concern throughout much of New England. Those who sought to further the influence of the revivals set about founding independent seminaries wherever the force of the revivals was felt. The pro-revival forces learned—to their dismay—that a Unitarian was named to a key professorship and the presidency at Harvard, and in response they formed a three-year, postcollegiate institution at Andover, Massachusetts in 1808. Andover, they believed, would counter the influence of the liberals at Harvard and prepare a new generation of pastors to continue the work of the revival in the churches. Andover, the first school to be called a "theological seminary,"[2] set the pattern for scores of seminaries that were to follow. The Presbyterians soon followed with the establishment of Princeton University in 1812.

The work of United Methodist forebears did not flourish in the centers of learning in the eastern United States. The Methodist, The Evangelical Association, and The United Brethren work was focused upon converting unbelievers and spreading scriptural holiness across the face of the growing frontier. These bodies gave of themselves. It is said that in the middle of the nineteenth century half of the circuit riders died before the age of thirty-five, and two-thirds died before they had completed twelve years of service.[3] Late in his life, the Baptist John Broadus voiced his keen respect for the Episcopalians and the Presbyterians with their fine educational programs, but then he added:

> But if it hadn't been for the great Methodist and great Baptist bodies, and some others like them, who have encouraged men to preach that were destitute of this artificial course of training, what in the world would have become of the masses of the people?[4]

Truth and Tradition

Methodists' early concern for education was expressed in a manner that conformed to their evangelistic mission. At the first General Conference of the Methodist preachers in the new world, the "Christmas Conference" in Baltimore, 1784, the preachers were admonished to read the tracts of Mr. Wesley and the British Methodist theologian John Fletcher. Mornings were to be given to five hours of study and prayer. Those who had no taste for such intensive study were encouraged to acquire the taste or return to their former employment![5]

In the years that followed, the Course of Study became more formally established as a responsibility of the bishops. They were to assure that no perverse doctrines from overseas were preached and that the preachers under their appointment taught solid Wesleyan teachings. In 1816 the General Conference developed a list of books and study guides that formed the Course of Study required of the Methodist preachers and printed them in the *Discipline* of the denomination.[6]

Of at least equal importance with the formally established Course of Study, however, was the informal instruction given to the circuit riders by their elders. The Methodist preachers were itinerants, unless age or ill health required them to remain in one place. This itinerant, circuit-riding ministry provided a means of theological education, as well as an astute method for preaching throughout the frontier. Younger preachers rode with experienced preachers, and as they rode together over great distances, they taught and learned by question and answer. The younger preacher observed the circuit rider fulfill his work and quizzed him on his approach. As the learner was able, he began to share the preaching responsibilities and received the benefit of the elder's critique. It was a system adapted well to the need.[7]

The need for more formal education became evident to the Methodists, however, as the frontier became settled

Context and Concern

and the preachers were assigned to a single congregation. The Methodists, no longer new converts and themselves often offspring of Methodist converts, were increasingly of the middle class and educated. The unlettered circuit rider was no longer adequate to the task of nurturing an educated church membership in the Christian faith. Methodist leaders began to argue that uneducated preachers could not command the respect of middle-class congregations, and they feared that the Methodists would have no choice but to abandon their denomination and join other congregations with a better educated clergy.

Many of the preachers themselves shared this same dissatisfaction with their level of education. The Reverend Peter Borein is a good example. Born in 1809 to an illiterate farming family in east Tennessee, Borein was converted as a young man and called into the preaching ministry. He did not even know the alphabet, but he set about trying to educate himself to read in English and Hebrew. His preaching was powerful, and he was assigned to become the pastor of Clark Street Methodist Church in Chicago (now First United Methodist, Chicago Temple). He spoke often to Mrs. Eliza Garrett, wife of the mayor of the city and member of his congregation, concerning his dismay at his lack of formal education. It was she who in 1853 became the leading figure in establishing a seminary bearing her husband's name, the second Methodist seminary established in the United States.[8]

The establishment of seminaries, however, was by no means the first or the most popular choice to prepare pastoral leadership for the new situation facing Methodists in the early decades of the nineteenth century. Following the settlement of the frontier, many of the churches, including Methodist, established liberal arts colleges in the expectation that they would be a powerful force in preparing both clergy and laity for professional life.[9]

Truth and Tradition

This approach, one long followed in the eastern United States, received the support of those who in no way would have favored the establishment of seminaries. Though attending college was not a requirement for ordination, some of the preachers, it was thought, could profit from studying the liberal arts in the company of the future physicians, lawyers, and teachers with whom they would serve. This development furthered the vision of the preacher arising from the people, called of God for a special calling, and well equipped to relate to the middle class.

Randolph-Macon was established by the Methodists in Virginia in 1822, and a number of similar institutions soon followed: Allegheny and Dickinson in Pennsylvania, McKendree in Illinois, Emory and Wesleyan in Georgia, and Indiana Asbury (later to become DePauw) in Indiana. These colleges were established at least in part to provide training for future ministers and to make it unnecessary for them to attend colleges supported by other denominations, where they would be exposed to alien doctrines and perhaps be induced to leave the denomination altogether. Possession of a college degree enhanced the standing of a preacher, and ownership of colleges became a mark of pride for the denomination.

It should not be supposed, however, that a denomination so accustomed to circuit riders warmed overnight to the idea of pastors with college degrees. Church members wanted their pastors to be presentable to a middle-class congregation and the community surrounding them, but at the same time they wanted to avoid any appearance of elitism. The Indiana Conference supported the formation of Indiana Asbury College (DePauw), for example, but the first graduate of the new college to join the conference, Thomas Goodwin, fell victim to the suspicion of some that college graduates would receive favorable appointments. In order to demonstrate the contrary, presiding elders consistently appointed Goodwin to the most mar-

18

Context and Concern

ginal places until Goodwin left in frustration and served the church as an editor.[10]

Even with these sentiments, however, there were those in the church who believed that some further training beyond liberal arts was required if pastors in the settled congregations were to provide adequate nurture to their members. John Dempster, a presiding elder in the Cayuga District of the Oneida Conference in New York (later Central New York), found that the unlettered and untrained preachers with whom he served were not capable of nurturing the new converts who were coming into the churches. He wrote Bishop Elijah Hedding asking him to assign men to come to help in this demanding work. When Bishop Hedding responded that there were no such leaders to be spared, Dempster resolved that better training should be provided. With others he helped form (1839), and staff the biblical institute at Newbury (Vermont) that later became the New England Biblical Institute (Concord, New Hampshire), and which, when it moved to Boston (1869), became the founding institution of Boston University. Dempster thought it was offensive to "sanction that degrading maxim of fancied infallibility that ignorance is the mother of devotion."[11] He argued the case for theological education before the General Conference of 1856.

Just a few years earlier, Dempster had journeyed west to the rapidly growing city of Chicago and began discussions with Mrs. Garrett and with other fellow Methodists, and these discussions led to the establishment of Garrett Biblical Institute, located on the campus of the new university taking shape, Northwestern University. Dempster resigned from the presidency of Garrett Biblical Institute, and at the time of his death he was journeying to the Pacific coast in the hope of establishing a seminary there.[12]

Dempster and his colleagues registered their successes in the face of a general opposition to seminary education among Methodists as a whole. The Evangelical Association shared this opposition. It published a four-year Course of Study for ministerial candidates in 1844. The General Conference of The Evangelical Association in 1847 took up the question of seminaries and resolved to study the question further. Despite assurances by the bishops that this seminary would be no "preacher factory," the proposal was turned down decisively. Later the association relented enough to allow conferences to establish educational institutions, but strictly ruled that they were not to be theological schools. Theological seminaries, it was thought, would expose future preachers to heresy and divide the ministry of the church into two castes.[13]

Even the first two seminaries formed among the Methodists were given birth with something less than resounding support of the denomination. The Newbury Biblical Institute was located in New England, an area that by then had a long tradition of clergy training, but it was not in a center of large Methodist membership.

The second seminary, Garrett Biblical Institute, took shape around the resolve of determined church leaders and the largesse of Mrs. Garrett. The editors of the *Northwestern Christian Advocate* learned of the plan to start a seminary and opined that it was "done in a corner."[14] The questions notwithstanding, the seminary soon received a state charter and the support of the Rock River, Illinois, Michigan, and North West Indiana Annual Conferences. In 1856, three years after it was chartered by the state of Illinois, Dempster and others represented the seminary at the General Conference. The conference acceded to the establishment of the seminary, but its action was clothed in language that, among other precautions: (1) required a call of God certified by a quarterly conference for admission; (2) protected against heresy in doctrine or slackness in discipline; (3) provided that trustees must always be members of the church and gave them oversight over the seminary; and (4) discouraged the

Context and Concern

multiplication of such institutions. One historian summarized the essence of the 1856 action in this way: "There they are. Let them be. Keep them under close leash."[15]

THE DEBATE OVER SEMINARIES

The debate over seminaries was joined somewhat later in the South than in the North, perhaps because the circuit rider system with its built-in form of apprenticeship training persisted longer in the southern church than it did in the North. The focus for southern discussion took place in the debates over the proposal in the southern church to form a central educational institution (later named Vanderbilt) for the training of future ministers. James Fraser has carefully traced the debates in 1872 that preceded the establishment of the university.[16] He warns that the opponents of theological seminaries cannot be dismissed simply as persons opposed to learning or progress. There were certain clear principles they had in mind that are important to hear not only for their insight into history but for interpreting concerns that persist to the present time.

Concerns for many centered in *doctrinal fidelity*. Institutions of learning were viewed as sources of heretical teaching capable of corrupting impressionable young men and creating confusion in the churches. Even after the establishment of Vanderbilt, Bishop George F. Pierce, one of the sturdiest foes of the action, said in 1879 to a group of new deacons:

> In these days, when the rage for education is so active and universal, I think our young preachers are in danger of adopting false views and wrong methods on the pretext of better preparation for their work. . . . We must teach sound doctrine—must sow the wheat of God's truth, not the chaff of human inventions.[17]

[handwritten: practical effectiveness was another concern.]

Truth and Tradition

A second cluster of concerns centered on *practical effectiveness*. Opponents of seminaries and college learning pointed out that preachers proved themselves by the fruits of their work. During the early days of the circuit rider, the preacher demonstrated his ability by preaching that moved audiences to repentance and conversion and by organizing the converts into congregations that preserved and enhanced the results of the revival. If the preacher was found wanting in such practical effectiveness, then, it was thought, no formal education could help him.

Even when more and more pastors were assigned to small circuits or stations, opponents of the seminaries argued that the apprenticeship system and the Course of Study were proven methods for preparing pastors and should not be replaced by more formal schooling.

Proponents of the seminary, as we have seen, also argued on the grounds of results. The nurture of souls and a settled ministry to an educated congregation simply could not be sustained, so they argued, by a preacher who himself was unlettered.

A third theme in the debates was the *distinctiveness of the Methodist movement*. The Methodists had followed the frontier west and had become the largest denomination in the country. It was argued that the Methodist preachers understood thoughts and feelings and language of the common people, and these masses had, under the providence of God, become the means of evangelizing the nation. When proponents of seminaries argued that sons and daughters of Methodists were going to other denominations because their pastors were better educated, their adversaries responded that they should be allowed to go if formal learning were the matter of first importance to them.

At stake in this debate was whether the Methodist movement was to remain an evangelistic force or to become a middle-class denomination like the other denomi-

Context and Concern

nations whose ministerial education it sought to emulate. For the preachers the issue at stake was whether they were called to a preaching and evangelizing office or to be prepared like lawyers and physicians to become members of an established profession.

A key element in all the discussions was the centrality and indispensability of *Christian experience*. It went without saying that an authentic call from God, confirmed by the church, was an absolutely essential prerequisite for any preacher. But the concern went further. Some held that the aim of Christian preaching was to share a powerful experience so effectively through the power of the Holy Spirit that the hearers would be moved to make this experience of forgiveness and redemption their own. Their opposition to the seminaries was not a matter of renouncing reason. They were no more prepared to dispense with reason than John Wesley. Their conviction was that unless one had the experience of faith and forgiveness as a foundation, then one's reason had no ground upon which to operate. With that ground, as the success of the frontier revivals had amply demonstrated, a literary education was unnecessary.

THE CONTEXT FOR PRESENT CONVERSATION

The early conversations and debates on theological education just recounted occurred in a denomination that had experienced significant change and dislocation. Church people were faced with the need to reexamine their identity, their future, and the leadership they would need. Contemporary discussions take place also in a time of great dislocation and uncertainty about identity as a church. It is understandable that we—no less than our forebears—struggle with some earnestness to reestablish our identity, discern the future, and consider the kind of

Truth and Tradition

leadership the church will need. The following paragraphs outline some of the wider questions that form the context for discussion on theological education today.

The Middle Class

Methodists who elected formal theological education in the nineteenth century placed their denomination in the "mainstream" of American life, the heart of the middle class. It is natural that a stress upon education and frugality should develop a constituency identified with the middle class and virtually indistinguishable from it. This perhaps served the church well when there was a large middle class with a unified set of values and vision for the country, but the dominant movements of recent history have been far from unifying or confirming for the middle class. Martin Marty has observed that our tendency until perhaps the 1960s was to think centripetally, and we exemplified this movement toward the center by unifying efforts, including the United Nations, the National Council of Churches, and even the earlier stages of the civil rights movement. The latter part of the century, however, is marked by centrifugal movement, movement toward particularity and separation.[18]

We are now a pluralistic nation, and we are—or soon will be—a nation of minorities. Culturally, there is no single great middle class to and for which a denomination may speak. Sociologists speak of a cultural left and a cultural right in American life with a disappearing middle.[19] Peter Berger holds that the middle class itself is divided into the more traditional managerial and industrial mind-sets and the growing body of information workers (including a whole array of professionals working in communications, financial services, various forms of therapy, etc.). The denominations, he holds, are largely constituted by the former, and the clergy disproportionately

[handwritten: The Middle class has changed]

represent the latter.[20] If our society in the nineteenth century was kindly disposed toward organized religions, we inherit today a mentality to which Stephen Carter has applied his now famous phrase, "the culture of disbelief."[21]

The middle class that the denomination chose to join in the nineteenth century is now disappearing or radically changed. This change itself prompts questions similar to those raised more than a century earlier concerning doctrine, identity, ministry, and theological education.

The Denomination

If the middle class has changed, so has the church that has identified with it so extensively. In the middle of the nineteenth century, the Methodist, United Brethren, and Evangelical denominations were growing evangelistic movements. They, along with the Baptists, stood distinct from the traditional denominations.

Now that The United Methodist Church is one of the mainstream denominations, it is no longer certain about its identity and distinctive mission. Furthermore, the denomination faces the fact that denominations and independent groups theologically more conservative (and with less history in formal theological education) are in many cases growing rapidly. The heirs of the circuit riders, by contrast, are diminishing in size, along with other traditional denominations.

Changing Mind-set

We can hardly speak of the changes confronting United Methodists at the close of the twentieth century without recognizing the demise of modernity itself. The perspective of the Enlightenment, formed out of the clash of religions in the Thirty Years' War in the early seventeenth century, now appears to be radically restructured or com-

Truth and Tradition

ing to an end. The massive changes now taking place are only partially understood. We do not know what will follow; therefore, we speak of "postmodern" times. Vaclav Havel, the president of the Czech Republic, recently spoke of the death of the era that presumably was going to be united by reason and science. Science, says Havel, is not able to explain the purpose of life to us. "Experts can explain anything in the objective world to us, yet we understand our own lives less and less.... By day," he concludes, "we work with statistics; in the evening, we consult astrologers."[22]

Other voices have discussed the demise of modernity at some length.[23] Our point at the moment is to notice that it is just those denominations that made some peace, however, uneasy, with the spirit of the Enlightenment that now are experiencing numerical decline. Denominations that never engaged in the struggle in the first place—unless it was to resist the encroachment of modernity—are in many cases experiencing rapid growth.

Typically, when a church faces turbulence and decline, there is a tendency to blame the predicament upon failure to adhere to ancient beliefs and practices. Those reacting in this manner, according to one observer, typically respond as follows:

> First they call for a return to the "old-time religion," the "ways of our fathers," and "respect for the flag." ... Second, they tend to find scapegoats in their midst ... upon whom they can project their fear; then, by punishing "outsiders" ... they can set an example of revived authority.... They are reactionaries who look backward to a golden time ... when the system worked; they insist that it will still work if only everyone will conform to the old standards.[24]

[Handwritten annotation at top: Persons say our problem caused by betrayal of present faith (Creeds!!, but not mentioned)]

Context and Concern

There are considerations in the present discussions that substantiate this analysis. In many discussions we hear parties blaming our present situation upon those who have betrayed the ancient faith. Often they promise that a return to some situation in the past will correct our failings and restore the church to its former power. For some, the seminaries and their alleged desertion of orthodoxy are the cause of decline. Others, only slightly more charitable, level blame at the seminaries because—whatever the source of our failing as a church—the seminaries have not acted effectively to correct it.

In conversations with church members, most will not assess blame, but they nonetheless voice serious concerns about the leadership of the future.[25] For example, the matter of *doctrinal fidelity and maintenance of discipline*, a prominent concern of the General Conference of 1856, remains a serious question for contemporary United Methodists. Seminary education exposes men and women to diverse theological and ethical perspectives. Voices of women, U.S. ethnic minorities, and Third World theologians—voices given little attention in previous generations—are now accorded a significant place in theological education. Members of congregations, annual conference boards of ordained and diaconal ministry, bishops, and others want to be assured that basic tenets of "classical Christian faith" are still taught and appropriated by present day students.

Furthermore, students now in seminary have grown up and attended college during and following the sexual revolution and have been exposed to significantly changed mores on sexual conduct and our understanding of issues related to human sexuality. In seminary they encounter the diversity of views on questions such as homosexuality that are prevalent in the wider church and society. While matters of sexual misconduct may have involved comparatively few clergy, the fact that they occur at all and

Truth and Tradition

the seriousness of the misconduct when it does occur have made the matter of discipline in one's personal and professional life a burning concern in many conferences. In such a context, United Methodist people naturally look to the seminaries to examine the discipline of the persons who are enrolled and the attention given to such matters while they are there. Doctrine and discipline remain key issues in any discussion of the seminaries among the churches.

The matter of *practical effectiveness* is also a concern in any discussion with the churches. Opponents of the seminaries in the middle of the nineteenth century argued that the revival was spread and sustained under the power of the Holy Spirit by persons who in most cases lacked formal education. Pragmatists that they were, they asked why the tradition should change what we were doing was working so well.

Today, any discussion of theological education with church leadership, lay and ordained, will involve in some way a concern about practical skills in ministry. Naturally, they seek women and men who can preach the Word, but concerns expressed reach much further. Knowing how to relate effectively with people, empowering lay people, moral and ethical leadership, spiritual formation, managing finances, leading in stewardship programs, working with youth, calling in the homes—these and many more aptitudes and skills are uppermost in the minds of lay people today.

Another area of concern for contemporary United Methodists, as well as for our forebears, relates to the *distinctiveness of the denomination*. More than a century ago, the predecessors of The United Methodist Church joined the middle class and in some sense became much like other Protestant denominations. In recent history, United Methodists have understood themselves so much a part of "mainline" Protestantism that they ask what it is that distinguishes them from others.

Context and Concern

United Methodists therefore are asking whether the seminaries are preparing clergy to reflect the distinctive ethos of the denomination. They want pastors who can remind the church of its distinctive role, its history, its pattern of organization, and its mission for the future. This need is complicated in some ways by the significant percentage of pastors who have attended non–United Methodist seminaries and who, in many cases, have not grown up in The United Methodist Church, as noted in chapter 3.

In addition to these concerns, United Methodists want to be assured that seminary education prepares students to work with actual congregations and does not so imbue them with the preoccupations of academia that they will be incapable or uninterested in working with the men, women, and children who make up a typical Christian congregation.

Beyond these concerns, the focus upon *Christian experience* is as central for United Methodists today as it was for our forebears in the nineteenth century. Then they asked of a pastor whether he had a vital experience of God's grace and evidenced this grace in continuing Christian growth in holiness of life. While the vocabulary is changed, there is no less direct concern of the church today that women and men presenting themselves for ordination be persons who have appropriated the faith and are growing steadily in the experience of the presence of God in their lives.

Church members rightly sense that spiritual integrity is at the heart of the matter and that the finest education in the world cannot compensate for lack of this core requirement. Students regularly express a similar concern for themselves and their classmates, and they seek the help of the seminaries in resources that sustain them in personal growth and depth in the Christian life.

Truth and Tradition

CONVERSATIONS AMONG SEMINARY FACULTY MEMBERS

The present conversation in the church concerning theological education takes place in the context of an unprecedented volume of discussion and writing within the seminaries themselves on the question of theological education.[26] Even a few allusions to key themes addressed in these publications will disclose the widespread attention that is given to theological education from the theological faculties themselves and the way in which many of these concerns coincide with questions raised by the churches.

A primary focus in these writings has been *the unity and purpose of theological education.* Edward Farley stimulated the more recent debates on the subject by criticizing the tendency of seminaries to focus upon the functions of the religious professional. This "functionalism," as he calls it, relegates the study of Bible and theology to theoretical undertakings, which are then in some manner to be applied to a concrete situation in the parish. Each subject in the seminary becomes a separate academic field, and the only unity known is that found in their common purpose of helping the student function in the role of a pastor or teacher.

The real unifying element, Farley contends, should not be the functions of a religious professional, important though they are, but the discipline (he calls it "habitus") involved in the saving knowledge of God. The heart of theological education is "the personal, sapiential knowledge (understanding) which can occur when faith opens itself to reflection and inquiry."[27] Though differing on important points, David Kelsey concurs with Farley on the unifying aim of theological education. In his terms, it is "to seek to understand God more truly."[28]

Context and Concern

A second theme that virtually all the contributors to the debate agreed upon is the need for the seminary education to be more *closely linked with the congregations.* Joseph Hough and John Cobb insist upon the development of Christian identity as a fundamental aim of theological education. They are quick to add that Christian identity is not conferred upon a person as an isolated individual but as a person who is a part of a church, who is enmeshed in a historical and global context, and who as a part of the church is heir to an "internal history" formed by God's activity in history. The church learns its identity by telling and retelling the story of God's dealings with the church and the world. The church's mission and the consequent identity of the Christian come from internalizing that story as a part of one's personal history.[29]

The reference to the formation of Christian identity is a clue to Hough and Cobb's interest in *personal experience.* Though the means of expression have changed since the 1800s, the concern in their thought and that of many others centers on helping the future pastor to grow in her/his personal experience of God and the personal appropriation of that faith that involves the whole of life.

David Kelsey has contrasted the "Berlin" model of theological education, which has been so prevalent in the United States, to the much older "Athenian" model formed by the Greeks four centuries before Christ and embraced by the Christian church as its own pattern of learning for hundreds of years. This Athenian model includes a heavy emphasis upon the conversion of the learner to God and the development of a religious community as a part of the learning experience. We will have occasion to look further at these contrasting models in chapter 6.

A further concern coming from the ranks of theologians themselves has been the *social location* of the seminaries. When nineteenth-century forebears of the present United

Truth and Tradition

Methodist denomination originally expressed opposition to the formation of seminaries, they spoke of the affinity Methodist preachers enjoyed with the ordinary people who populated the frontier. They communicated with the people and understood their thoughts and feelings.

There are overtones of that concern in today's conversation with various forms of liberation and feminist theology. Contemporary concerns, of course, go far deeper than simple ability to communicate across social and educational barriers. Liberation theologians and feminist theologians insist that there is a distinctive perspective, a "special reading" of the experience of God, which oppressed people enjoy, and which should be the beginning point for the theological effort itself.

Gustavo Gutierrez, for example, a generation ago spoke of theology as the response of the whole person to the love of God. In view of the enormity of human suffering found around us, therefore, there is only one tenable location for the person of faith, and that is in solidarity with the poor in the work of liberation. This solidarity, Gutierrez held, is the core and first step of theology, and theology itself is critical reflection upon the involvement on the basis of the Word of God.[30] Similarly, James Cone designated the "life of humiliation and suffering" of the African American community as the point of departure for Black theology.[31]

Feminist theologians, following the lead of Rosemary Radford Ruether,[32] have reminded the church that theology has tended to view the experience of Caucasian men as normative and has dealt with all theological subjects from that perspective. The agenda of feminist theology has not only sought to correct this obvious distortion of theology; feminist theologians have attempted to reconceive the theological enterprise itself. The Mud Flower Collective, for example, wrote of the need to make the pursuit of justice for women and for other marginalized groups in our society the point of departure for theology.[33]

Rebecca Chopp likewise calls for a fundamental rethinking of theology, which, she holds, identifies objective knowledge with the masculine and private religion with the feminine.[34] Feminist theology, according to Chopp, should not confine itself to reform of present theological structures but should reconstruct the dwelling itself.[35]

The concerns of these liberation and feminist theologians spring from perspectives strikingly different from voices in the 1800s who were pleading for closer identification with the common people and protesting against the contaminating effects of higher education. There are nonetheless some common elements between the two. Both plead for a special insight or beginning point to be realized by locating oneself with a particular group of people. Both believe that the task of theology is to further the work of God in saving, redeeming, and liberating the people who themselves are the servants of salvation to others.

These brief allusions give some sense of the basic and formative questions being raised from the seminary community itself. In important ways, these concerns of faculty members and administrators themselves parallel the issues raised by the wider circle of lay people in the churches.

* * *

We have sought to set the context for this discussion by illustrating the manner in which significant changes in church and society require the church to rethink its mission and therefore to reconsider the leadership needed and the means by which it may be prepared. The chapters that follow will look carefully at some of the core questions involved in the church's conversation on the future of theological education. The concluding chapter suggests some of the themes that need to inform theological education for the years immediately ahead.

Truth and Tradition

NOTES

1. Quoted in James W. Fraser, *Schooling the Preachers: The Development of Protestant Theological Education in the United States 1740–1875* (New York: University Press of America, 1988), 3.
2. Ibid., 34.
3. William K. Anderson, ed., *Methodism* (Kansas City: The Methodist Publishing House, 1947), 167. Cited by Donald E. Messer, "Where Do We Go from Here?" in *Send Me: The Itinerancy in Crisis*, ed. Donald E. Messer (Nashville: Abingdon Press, 1991), 159.
4. John A. Broadus, "Ministerial Education," in *Sermons and Addresses* (Baltimore: H. M. Wharton & Co., 1887), 201-2, as quoted in Fraser, *Schooling the Preachers*, 79.
5. Gerald O. McCulloh, *Ministerial Education in the American Methodist Movement* (Nashville: United Board of Higher Education and Ministry, 1980), 10-11.
6. Ibid., 12.
7. Fraser, *Schooling the Preachers*, 89.
8. Ila Alexander Fisher, "Eliza Garrett: To Follow a Vision," in *Spirituality and Social Responsibility: Vocational Vision of Women in The United Methodist Tradition*, ed. Rosemary Skinner Keller (Nashville: Abingdon Press, 1993), 43.
9. See Glenn T. Miller, *op. cit.*, 205.
10. Fraser, *Schooling the Preachers*, 113.
11. *Northwest Christian Advocate*, IV (July 2, 1856) as quoted in Frederick A. Norwood, *Dawn to Midday at Garrett* (Evanston: Garrett-Evangelical Theological Seminary, 1978), 9.
12. McCulloh, *Ministerial Education*, 31.
13. Paul H. Eller, "Evangelical Theological Seminary," in *The Seminary Review*: LIX:92 (Spring 1973), 12-13.
14. *Northwestern Christian Advocate*, II (February 8, 1854): 26 as quoted in Norwood, *Dawn to Midday*, 14.
15. Norwood, *Dawn to Midday*, 19. The resolutions are printed in the *Journal of General Conference, 1856*, 150-51.
16. Fraser follows the debate in his *Schooling the Preachers*, 123-50.
17. From his "Character and Work of a Gospel Minister," delivered October 26, 1879 in Abingdon, Virginia. Quoted in Fraser, *Schooling the Preachers*, 133.
18. See Martin Marty, "From the Centripetal to the Centrifugal in Culture and Religion," *Theology Today* 51:1 (April 1994): 6.
19. See Wade Clark Roof, "America's Voluntary Establishment: Mainline Religion in Transition," in Mary Douglas and Steven Tipton, eds., *Religion and America: Spiritual Life in a Secular Age* (Boston: Beacon Press, 1983), 130-49. See also Tex Sample, *U.S. Lifestyles and Mainline Churches* (Louisville: Westminster/John Knox Press, 1990), 99-138.
20. *A Far Glory: The Quest for Faith in an Age of Credulity* (New York: The Free Press, 1992).
21. Stephen L. Carter, *The Culture of Disbelief: How American Law and Politics Trivialize Religious Devotion* (New York: BasicBooks, 1993).
22. Taken from an address by Vaclav Havel in Philadelphia, July, 1994. Reported in Nicholas Wade, "Method and Madness," in *New York Times Magazine*, 14 August 1994, 18.

23. See, for example, Albert Bormann, *Crossing the Postmodern Divide* (Chicago: University of Chicago Press, 1992). *See also* Stephen Toulmin, *Cosmopolis: The Hidden Agenda of Modernity* (New York: Free Press, 1990).
24. William Gerald McLoughlin, *Revivals, Awakenings, and Reform* (Chicago: University of Chicago Press, 1978), 14 as quoted in Martin Marty, "Revitalized Religion," in *Christian Century*, 102:22 (July 3-10, 1985): 650-52.
25. Many formal and less formal conversations have occurred with church leaders, both clergy and lay. In the spring of 1994, the presidents and deans of the thirteen United Methodist seminaries (the Association of United Methodist Theological Schools) engaged in Agenda 21: United Methodist Ministry for a New Century, directed by Donald H. Treese and supported by the Board of Higher Education and Ministry of The United Methodist Church. The project involved about seven hundred laity and clergy at thirteen regional events. Those events provided significant opportunity for extended conversation on concerns related to theological education. Those conversations were carefully recorded and compiled. A draft of the report has been used as a general background in compiling this section.
26. Some of the prominent titles issued as a part of this extensive discussion include Edward Farley, *Theologia: The Fragmentation and Unity of Theological Education* (Philadelphia: Fortress Press, 1983) and *The Fragility of Knowledge: Theological Education in the Church and the University* (Philadelphia: Fortress Press, 1988); Joseph C. Hough, Jr. and John B. Cobb, Jr., *Christian Identity and Theological Education* (Chico, Calif.: Scholars Press, 1988); David H. Kelsey, *Between Athens and Berlin: The Theological Education Debate* (Grand Rapids: William B. Eerdmans, 1993) and *To Understand God Truly: What's Theological about a Theological School* (Louisville: Westminster/John Knox Press, 1992); Mary Elizabeth Moore, *Teaching from the Heart: Theology and Educational Method* (Minneapolis: Fortress Press, 1991); The Mud Flower Collective, *God's Fierce Whimsy: Christian Feminism and Theological Education* (New York: Pilgrim Press, 1985); Charles M. Wood, *Vision and Discernment: An Orientation in Theological Study* (Atlanta: Scholars Press, 1985); Max L. Stackhouse, ed., *Apologia: Contextualization, Globalization and Mission in Theological Education* (Grand Rapids: William B. Eerdmans, 1988). Among other collections of essays see *Ecumenical & Interreligious Perspectives: Globalization in Theological Education*, ed. Russell E. Richey (Nashville: Board of Higher Education and Ministry, United Methodist Church, 1992); *The Education of the Practical Theologian: Responses to Joseph Hough and John Cobb's Christian Identity and Theological Education*, ed. Don S. Browning (Atlanta: Scholars Press, 1989); *Theological Education and Moral Formation*, ed. Richard John Neuhaus (Grand Rapids: William B. Eerdmans, 1992); and *Shifting Boundaries: Contextual Approaches to the Structure of Theological Education*, ed. Barbara G. Wheeler and Edward Farley (Louisville: Westminster/John Knox Press, 1991). As this book went to press the editor had opportunity to see portions of the manuscript for Donald E. Messer, *Calling Church & Seminary into the 21st Century*. (Nashville: Abingdon, 1995).
27. Farley, *Theologia*, 156.
28. David Kelsey, *To Understand God Truly*, 15.
29. Hough and Cobb, *Christian Identity and Theological Education*, 19-48.

Truth and Tradition

30. Gustavo Gutierrez, *A Theology of Liberation: History, Politics, and Salvation*, trans. Sister Caridad Inda and John Eagleson (Maryknoll, N.Y.: Orbis Books, 1973), 6, 7, and 11.
31. James H. Cone, *A Black Theology of Liberation* (Philadelphia: J. B. Lippincott Company, 1970), 12.
32. Rosemary Reuther, *Liberation Theology* (New York: Paulist Press, 1970).
33. Mud Flower Collective, *God's Fierce Whimsy: Christian Feminism and Theological Education* (New York: Pilgrim Press, 1985).
34. Rebecca Chopp, "Situating the Structure: Prophetic Feminism and Theological Education," in *Shifting Boundaries: Contextual Approaches to the Structure of Theological Education*, ed. Barbara G. Wheeler and Edward Farley (Louisville: Westminster/John Knox Press, 1991), 80f.
35. Rebecca S. Chopp, *The Power to Speak: Feminism, Language, God* (New York: Crossroad, 1989), 22. *See also* contributions by Elisabeth Schussler Fiorenza, "Theological Education: Biblical Studies," 1-20, and Rebecca Chopp, "When the Center Cannot Contain the Margins," 63-76, in *The Education of the Practical Theologian*, ed. Don S. Browning (Atlanta: Scholars Press, 1989).

Chapter Two

Truth and Tradition

Robert C. Neville

All important issues in the church need to be anchored in theological reflection, and this is especially true of matters pertaining to Christian ministry, education, and leadership. Accordingly, this chapter will begin with a theological statement of some of the main conditions relating Christian truth to its theological traditions, focusing on those relevant to the shaping of tradition in new situations. It will then move to the specifically Wesleyan theological tradition which is especially rich and resourceful among American denominational movements for nourishing ancient traditional roots in new fields of endeavor. The current situation for American theological education will then be sketched as a complex mission field to which the gospel's traditions should be addressed, including not only the conditions of American Christianity but also the conditions of Christian movements around the globe, whose leaders come to our seminaries for training. Finally, the conflicting agendas among different groups in theological education will be shown to be not so much disagreements on the items but on the priorities, from which follow very different ways of identifying with Christian traditions.

Truth and Tradition

A THEOLOGY OF TRUTH AND TRADITION

The purpose of academic Christian theological education is to prepare leaders for the Christian movement in ways appropriate for academic learning. Many other things leaders should know have to come from their own experience, from directly engaging the ongoing issues of the Christian community and its needs, and from the cultivation of their own spiritual lives. To expect much from seminaries in these matters is to misdirect attention from the proper roles of churches in the education of their leaders. But academic learning is indeed relevant to identifying the gospel and understanding how it should be addressed to the needs of the situation. Both the nature of Christian truth and the relevant ways of appropriating tradition are central topics of academic theological education and among the central reasons for the Methodist emphasis on learned ministry.

Christian truth has to do with understanding the teachings and life of Jesus and the significance of both for salvation. This necessarily includes but is not limited to the knowledge of the Bible in its place and time. In addition, the salvific significance of Jesus needs to be interpreted and expressed for the various conditions of our own places and time. Christian truth is not only about history but about those things that can transform persons and situations in the present so as to bring about more nearly the kingdom of God.

Perhaps it is misleading to say that Christian truth is about Jesus and his saving power. Jesus lived within a wider world of assumptions, some of which he mentioned at length, for instance, the importance of the kingdom of God, the meaning of messiahship, and so forth. Other points he merely assumed or mentioned in passing, for instance, that God is creator of the world, of all nature, and lord of human history, and that evil is a force to be

Truth and Tradition

combated. These latter assumptions were not peculiar to Christianity or to Jesus' own life but were widespread through Jewish and Hellenistic culture; they are not "Christian truths" but are necessary to grasp as the context for what is more peculiarly Christian. Beyond these are assumptions common to most or all religions that are necessary for making sense of religion as such, for instance, that the human condition is to be under obligation, that people frequently if not nearly always fail that obligation, and that something out of the ordinary, such as divine intervention, is necessary to do something about that. To understand Christian truth requires attending not only to what is peculiarly Christian but to the entire cultural and metaphysical context that is presupposed in making sense of the salvific significance of Jesus' life.

Just as the larger cultural and metaphysical context of Jesus' time is necessary for grasping the gospel, the larger cultural, historical, and philosophical conditions of our own time need to be understood in order to see how the gospel can having saving power now. This means learning what the social sciences can tell us about our neighborhoods, our economies, our political institutions, and the psychological states of various peoples. It means learning about the nature, history, and care of our world from the physical scientists. It means learning from the artists and writers about the state of the souls of people in different conditions. It means learning from philosophers in all the cultures of the world where Christianity has a presence about the conditions of truth. Most of all, understanding the gospel in our situation requires being able to distinguish the assumptions and agendas of our social and physical sciences, our arts and philosophies, from assumptions appropriate to the gospel. The prophetic dimension of the gospel ought to be informed by but not reduced to the agendas of right-wing or left-wing social movements. The Christian acknowledgment that God is creator of the

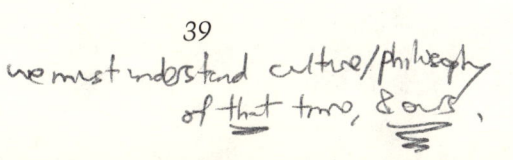

39

Truth and Tradition

cosmos ought to be informed by but not reduced to mere identification with some historical cause or with an ecological program. The gospel's interpretations of sin and spiritual life ought to be informed by but not reduced to moral critiques and pastoral psychology.

The critical discernment of the expression of the gospel in relation to culture is vastly complex. The process needs to resist the siren calls for simplicity that usually result in either losing the gospel in the excitements of culture or adopting a historic expression of the gospel that addresses some other culture than the one that is our mission field. The people who most need to be able to discern the saving word of the gospel for their time are our leaders, and easy to understand why seminary curricula have become so packed as they have attempted to prepare leaders in the critical discernment of the gospel.

How do we know that we understand the gospel and its proper expression? The classic Methodist answer is, through Wesley's quadrilateral: scripture, tradition, reason, and experience. Each is both a special source of knowledge and a check or help for understanding the others. Since Wesley's day we have greatly increased many of our capacities for understanding scripture, through finding more ancient texts, developing new techniques of analysis, and having a better historical and sociological grasp of biblical times. Our knowledge of Christian traditions has been augmented by anthropological and musicological studies of traditions of liturgy and practice, and also by recognition of traditions of Christian life outside the stretch of European Christendom that formed Wesley's world. *Reason* means many things in theology, from hermeneutics to casuistry to philosophy to criticism. *Experience,* for Wesley, usually meant experience of the presence of God, which is closely connected with understanding the Holy Spirit. Now that rubric of theological experience has been expanded to include recognition of

Truth and Tradition

the diverse ways different kinds of people experience the same phenomenon; this point arose over a century ago in recognition of the different experiences of persons in foreign missions but now has been applied to the experiences of women, minorities, and other groups whose perspectives had not been given much articulation or credence.

These four "sides" to the quadrilateral offer different kinds of evidence and judgment concerning the gospel. How these are balanced and integrated at any one time is itself a matter of tradition. For instance, Protestants and Roman Catholics at the time of the Reformation and Counter-Reformation had distinctly different weightings of scripture and tradition, respectively; the weightings are far more similar now. Pentecostal traditions give far more weight to experience relative to tradition, scripture, and reason, than most other traditions. Traditions dominated by scholasticism, such as fourteenth-century European Christianity or seventeenth-century Protestant orthodoxy, give great weight to reason. Traditions nowadays deeply informed by one or another liberation theology give weight to experience in the contemporary sense.

Whether to speak of *the* Christian tradition or Christian *traditions* in the plural is a complicated question. In one sense, the Christian tradition is the vast complex of cultural transformations by which the saving power of the gospel is carried to wherever it goes. In another sense, we should recognize the great variations and divergencies among Christian traditions. The three great communions of the Nicean and Chalcedonian creeds—Orthodoxy, Roman Catholicism, and Protestantism—are out of communion with one another, and the three together are alienated even more from the Monophysite churches, such as that in Coptic Egypt and Ethiopia. Furthermore, there are distinct differences over time, as between the ancient, medieval, and modern traditions of European Christianity. Moreover, living religious communities

Truth and Tradition

> Appeal to "tradition" is usually to one or another of the traditions, often relative to another tradition

have semiautonomous minitraditions coexisting and interacting, such as abstract theological traditions, liturgical and musical traditions, ethical and political traditions, and so on. When theological appeals are made to tradition, they nearly always are to one or another of these diverse traditions, segments of tradition, or minitraditions, and the appeals are made in contradistinction to the influence of some other traditional part. Sometimes it is best to speak of *tradition,* and sometimes of *traditions,* but the ambiguities need to be borne in mind.

Traditions are never authoritative simply by themselves as they stand. They are always changing to adapt to new circumstances. The gospel is always in the process of being retranslated to address conditions it had not addressed before. The interpretation of scripture, the fresh knowledge coming from experience, and the rational imagination of reason, are all involved in restructuring and reappropriating tradition. A tradition is a growing thing whose most proximate embodiment is malleable and ever undergoing reformation. As each age and condition of the church needs to reappropriate Christian traditions to make them its own, the traditions themselves are in flux and need to be guided responsibly in their development.

When conditions of society and the church change so fast that both are troubled by questions of their identity, goals, and even of their true origins, there is a great temptation to appeal to tradition itself to settle the questions. Thomas C. Oden, for instance, in a recent popular article bathetically titled "Confessions of a Grieving Seminary Professor," attributes the "political indiscretions, sexual escapades, and ideological binges" of parish pastors to the triumph of "modernity" in seminaries.[1] By modernity here he means "a tradition-deprived seminary ethos," lack of "classical Christian texts," failure to transmit "the apostolic tradition," the systematic blocking out

Truth and Tradition

of "ancient ecumenical teaching," and the abandonment of a concern to identify heresies.[2] Although there is not much conceptual clarity in this popular article, Oden is a distinguished seminary professor at Drew who has written a three-volume systematic theology that provides more than enough clarity for his point. In the preface to volume 1, *The Living God*, Oden says that his task is to do systematic theology in the context of the collapse of modernity (p. x) and that his specific purpose "is to set forth an ordered view of the faith of the Christian community upon which there has generally been substantial agreement between the traditions of East and West, including Catholic, Protestant, and Orthodox."[3] His purpose "is to listen single-mindedly for the voice of that deeper, ecumenical consensus that has been gratefully celebrated as received teaching by believers of vastly different cultural settings—whether African or European, Eastern or Western, sixth or sixteenth century" (p. ix). He writes of the "central Christian tradition," the "ancient ecumenical consensus of Christian teaching of God (cf. credal summaries of Irenaeus, c. 190, Tertullian, c. 200, Hippolytus, c. 215, Council of Caesarea, 325, Council of Nicaea, 325, Marcellus, 340, Cyril of Jerusalem, 350, Council of Constantinople, 381, Rufinus, 404, Council of Chalcedon, 451. . .) that still embraces and empowers not only centrist Protestants and traditional Roman Catholics and Orthodox, but also great numbers of evangelicals, liberals, and charismatics" (p. ix).

Whereas it is splendid to have a major United Methodist theologian advocating greater attention to the traditions of the creedal period in European Christianity, such appeals to specific parts of the tradition as a criticism of current practice are not sufficient by themselves and dangerous if not used with great care. There are at least three senses in which this kind of appeal to tradition is deceptive.

[Margin note: 1st, "excluded" communities must be heard.]

Truth and Tradition

[Margin: ★] First, any attempt to say what part of the overall Christian tradition or which tradition among the many that have shaped Christian communities is "central" or normative must give a thorough hearing to the excluded traditions in order to be fair. And if equal time is given to the excluded traditions, what is to be gained by the specific appeal to the "central" tradition except to say we could learn from ancient sources? The tradition Professor Oden cites defined itself by excluding the Arians, most of whom were Goths rather than Greeks or Romans; was there a good theological reason for this that still bears on current concerns, or was it part of the politics of empire? Oden's tradition also defined itself by excluding the Monophysites who believed in "one nature" for Christ rather than "two natures," although Oden's central tradition was never able to say persuasively how Christ could have two natures; how much of that "central" tradition took shape because so many of the Monophysites were Persians with political loyalty there rather than to Rome or Byzantium? *[Margin: ★]* Central to that "central" tradition was the exclusion of women from positions of authority in the church and the construction of a church organization on hierarchical lines. Is this to be affirmed by citing the authority of that creedal tradition to correct the abuses of modernism?

Second, that segment of the Christian tradition to which Professor Oden calls attention was precisely the part that was downplayed and subordinated by Luther and Calvin in shaping the Protestant tradition. The Protestant tradition gives greater emphasis to the traditions of the biblical period and to the experience of contemporary people. The Anglicans from which Wesley came were less vociferous in subordinating the traditions of the creedal period than other Protestants, but what Wesley appreciated from that period was not the creedal statements and *[Margin: ?]* heresy hunts but the experiential explications of the process of holiness in the Cappadocian fathers, for instance.

44

Professor Oden's appeal to the part of the tradition he lifts up seems on the face of it to be a reversal, if not betrayal, of the Protestant tradition that more immediately defines the Methodist heritage.

Third, however enlightening they are, the creedal traditions of the ancient world simply do not address the new issues that have arisen with modernity. They give no guidance whatsoever concerning how the gospel is to be expressed in a world shaped by modern science, by the modern historical consciousness, by democratic sensibilities, by meritocratic societies, by advanced technologies, or by moral, political, and spiritual critiques of Christianity in its imperial cultural mode that it obtained during much of the ancient creedal period. In these respects the traditions of the ancient church are too innocent to be helpful regarding the correction of the abuses of modernity. The direct application of them to situations their shapers never envisioned, without careful reconstruction in light of the problems of modernity, would be disingenuous authoritarianism. Only the traditions that have developed through the modern period, reinterpreting the creedal traditions to be sure, are likely to have much to help express the gospel's stance toward modernity.

None of this is to say that Protestants do not have much to learn from the ancient traditions of the European church in its creeds. Nor is it to say that the modern interpreters of those traditions, such as Adolf Harnack, were correct. It is only to say that an appeal to some tradition, to some part of the mix of traditions within Christianity, in order to criticize current practice needs to be justified by considerations of scripture, experience, and reason as well as by consideration of the traditions to which appeal is made and their alternatives.

These qualifications of the appeal to tradition having been made, it is important to reemphasize the point that there is no Christian truth without tradition. The tradi-

> The key: Does the tradition carry Gospel truth?

Truth and Tradition

tion is what carries down the saving love of God incarnate in Jesus, passed to the disciples, and then conveyed across many cultures, vast distances, and over a long time to us. But what is carried down is the gospel truth, the saving power, not any one expression in biblical or creedal form, not a medieval Summa nor a Protestant sermon or commentary. These are among the vehicles for the truth, along with hymns and liturgies, communal organizations and ethical practices, and countless other elements of living traditions. But the vehicles are never above criticism as to whether they carry the living waters.

THE WESLEYAN THEOLOGICAL TRADITION

Tradition within Methodism has been shaped decisively by John Wesley. Different aspects of Wesley's influence have been given expression by different parts of the Wesleyan movement, and at different times. There are three aspects that are particularly helpful for orienting theological education today: his emphases on sophisticated learning, on unitary holiness, and on evangelical outreach.

In contrast to most other eighteenth-century evangelical English reformers, Wesley loved sophisticated learning and saw no special tension between the gospel and either historical book-learning or the experimental learning of the Enlightenment. His movement began in Oxford University and, although he took it to people who would never set foot within an institution of higher education, it was always comfortable with intellectual sophistication. Wesley himself was no careful scholar. But he advocated learning for his people and edited and abridged classics and his own favorite spiritual writings for wide distribution. He was fascinated by new discoveries and science, especially medicine. If anything, he was too gullible concerning the curiosities of his day.[4] It is not surprising that his American followers, when they were out of touch with the English university establishment by virtue of great distance, founded institutions of higher education across the continent. American Methodist colleges and universities did not attempt to create a protective buffer for young Christians against a hostile world, as did so many other religious educational institutions, but sought to bring people of modest means and background into the wider world of intellect and learning. Again and again, Methodists have evangelized some downtrodden group or immigrant community and sent them to college, only to have them become middle-class. Whereas liberal Methodists today are somewhat embarrassed by the middle-class character of their churches, that is the happy and almost inevitable consequence of stressing education in religion, and that character should work in current mission areas. In this respect, Methodism is a thoroughly modern tradition. The implications for Methodist theological education are potent.

Wesley's emphasis on holiness was part of his evangelical orientation, and thus gave his movement a different stress from both the Anglican church within which he worked and the more confessionally oriented churches of the Reformation; it gave him an unusual affinity with Roman Catholics and with his vision of the Orthodox Cappadocian thinkers. What distinguished his concern with holiness from that of many other evangelicals was his insistence on unifying personal sanctification with the reform of social conditions, which today we would call social justice. Wesley did not merely believe in both personal sanctification and social justice. Rather, he believed that a person is to be identified not only with inner thoughts and feelings but also with behavior and public life. Therefore, it is impossible even to conceive of personal sanctification without asking what this means for

Truth and Tradition

the reformation of a person's social circumstances. Wesley's famous doctrine of perfection in this life is difficult in many respects, and he himself seemed to soften some of the stronger claims to little more than deathbed feelings of full consent to moral and spiritual law. But he never allowed a separation of inner holiness from outer works.

Wesley's unitary conception of personal and social holiness stands in contrast to the more common evangelical emphasis on personal holiness alone, an emphasis as common today as in his time. It also stands in contrast to the emphasis in liberal denominations on social justice with a bit of embarrassment about personal holiness. Sometimes United Methodism in America has tended to forget the connection with personal holiness in Wesley's unitary conception, but that has not been forgotten by the African American Methodist denominations, and some smaller offshoots, nor by the conferences of United Methodism outside North America. It is a continuing theme in American United Methodist seminary education. Appeal to Wesley's unitary holiness has a balancing effect in the contemporary situation in which concerns for spiritual life and social justice tend to diverge and polarize opposition.

Third, perhaps most important for our situation, was Wesley's attitude toward tradition relative to evangelization, namely, that Christian traditions are strong enough to be put at risk for the sake of reaching new people with the gospel. He was an Anglican and struggled all his life to remain loyal to that tradition. Yet he took the gospel to people whose culture was not in tune with Anglican sensibilities. He modified liturgies, rephrased theologies, and with his brother invented a new hymnody to meet the needs of people who were not reached by his unchanged inherited traditions. When his movement in America lacked leadership, he took the step of ordaining leaders

Truth and Tradition

that, by tradition, he could not do without being a bishop. In none of this did he extend or go beyond tradition because he thought tradition was unimportant. Rather, it was because he thought the heart of the tradition was strong enough that it could be modified to accomplish the communication of the gospel in saving truth and power.

Wesley's emphasis on risking tradition for evangelical outreach is extremely important for these times of rapid change in Christianity. It is not surprising that Methodists were among the first to risk patriarchal traditions to bring women into positions of leadership. Nor is it surprising that Methodists risk their connectional systems to bring the gospel to foreign-language communities, from the German communities of the nineteenth century to the Korean congregations of today. Nor is it surprising that Methodists have risked European forms of church life to embrace a diversely indigenized family of Methodist church bodies around the world, as gathered in the World Methodist Council.

In all these "risks" of tradition, the risk is real. Much can be lost, and nearly always there are pendulum swings of emphasis. As mentioned earlier, the strong Methodist commitment to social justice in North America, which reached its peak during the McCarthy era when there were penalties even for privileged white men to speak out, strained the tradition of unitary holiness and in some instances lost touch with personal spirituality. Perhaps the reason for this was the need for the Methodist social justice movement to build political allegiances with other religions and secular groups that also stood for social justice but who did not share the beliefs or rhetoric of personal Christian sanctity. The strong revival of spiritual formation in United Methodist seminaries today marks a compensatory swing of the pendulum.

The great issues at risk in the Wesleyan willingness to change and extend traditions for the sake of evangelical

Truth and Tradition

outreach testify to the importance of his emphasis on sophisticated learning, especially theological learning. How can we weigh the risks, minimize loss of integrity in the traditions, and initiate compensatory movements, when we do not understand what is at stake? Never has there been a time when religious leaders need more to be steeped in their theological and liturgical heritages and informed about the conditions to which those heritages need to be made relevant. Wesley would insist upon the point with which this chapter began, namely, that the gospel should be presented as true—not merely as historically accurate but as transformative with saving power. The point is not to be faithful to traditions per se but to extend the traditions to effectiveness in our current field of mission.

OUR MISSION FIELD

Other chapters in this volume explore the contemporary mission of the church in far greater detail than will be sketched here. The remarks in this section are intended only to prepare the way for the brief discussion of theological agendas in the following section. In many respects the mission of the church can be divided into two parts: ministering to people within the Christian movement who have taken on the life of discipleship and ministering to those outside. This is not a simple division, however, because, as Paul pointed out in 1 Corinthians, for instance, the life of the congregation itself should be to minister to the whole city. Furthermore, there are important differences among people involved with Christianity: some are serious disciples; some like the fellowship; some participate for cultural reasons; and, some participate because they do not know any better. And there are people outside

Truth and Tradition

the explicit movement who seem more Christian in character than many within.

In the context of this chapter, the field for Christian mission includes all those who need to hear the word of the gospel, or hear it again, or hear it in a new way, so as to advance in holiness both spiritually and as influences in the social environment. The character of this field is subject to changing historical, social, and spiritual conditions. Some of the obvious characteristics of the present situation are the following:

1. Women in all branches of Christendom long have heard an impoverished gospel regarding their standing in society, in the church, and before God. There is a desperate need to address a full gospel to women and, when this is done, it will effect the greatest change in Christianity in centuries. There are many conditions of women, rich and poor, educated and uneducated, of different races and ethnic groups, of different nationalities, and of different orientations toward social, economic, domestic, and sexual roles. A full gospel must be nuanced toward these and other differences as it long has been with regard to the different circumstances of men.

2. Related to the above, the contemporary mission field includes helping people both inside and outside the church relate to others who are very different from themselves. This is an ancient Christian theme, expressed dramatically in the story of the good Samaritan. But it has been ignored or suppressed and this has given rise to pernicious bigotry against those who are different, bigotry regarding race, sexual orientation, conditions of ill health or disablement, lifestyle, culture, and tradition. In historical periods characterized by little travel, poor communication, and social segregation, this aspect of the mission field might not have seemed important. It is important today. In all times it was important to the victims.

Truth and Tradition

3. There are many nations or parts of nations, even within the United States, where Christianity is a new religion. These cultures have not been affected previously by Christianity, and there are many open questions about what Christianity calls for. How much of traditional African religion needs to be abandoned or modified for African Christians? How should Korean Christians relate to their Buddhist relatives and their own Confucian sensibilities? These are frontline questions of mission for "new Christians," and they bring them to seminary.

4. What interpretation does Christianity offer concerning the nature of human life, the meaning or value of the cosmos, the issues of world politics, and the nature of spiritual fulfillment, that can be expressed to secular culture and to other interested religions? Christianity must have something to say about these and related things if it is to go on to offer a saving word. Sometimes it is possible to offer a saving word to an individual by focusing on the immediate concerns of the person's life; our common evangelism works this way. But immediate concerns are often not the most important ones. The Christian mission is to the world and people in all nations, and Christianity needs to be able to interpret that in a sophisticated way. In English-speaking countries, there seem to be few if any successors to C. S. Lewis and Paul Tillich for the task of expressing the Christian faith to the world.

5. Another, somewhat peculiar, characteristic of our current mission field is the assessment of our inherited institutions. So much energy of the Christian life goes into keeping our religious institutions going that the question inevitably arises as to whether the maintenance is all necessary. Two extremes are to be avoided. One is the instrumentalist view that church institutions are to be judged for their efficiency at accomplishing some purpose other than the exercise of life within them. True, some institutions are for the sake of goals other than them-

Truth and Tradition

selves. But other institutions, such as those of good community life, are fulfilled simply in being exercised as Christian ways to exist. The other extreme is the culture-religion view that Christianity is simply a cultural way of life whose customs should be supported for their own sake. As mentioned above, the Christian way of life consists in the pursuit of holiness in personal spirituality and in effective neighborliness. Among our neighbors are many non-Christians. Part of the Christian mission is to assess what is living and dead in our institutions.

6. Finally, there is a Christian mission to create more just social structures generally and to foster proper protection of and deference to the environment. The obligations to justice and nature are not peculiar to Christians: they are obligatory to anyone, and everyone ought to pursue social justice and practice deference to the environment. Also, the specific contents of these obligations differ from place to place; the proper balance of environmental and social concerns in Brazil is different from those in Washington state, and Christians need to act locally as well as to support larger causes. Despite the universality of obligation and the diversity of its content, Christians have a special obligation to attend to obligations. It is part of the covenant with God by which Christians understand their gospel. Christians, as Christians, ought not fail to engage their responsibilities which are also obligatory for everyone. This is not to minimize the difficulty in many circumstances of discerning what one is obligated to do—too often sentimental pieties get in the way of the severe discernment that true justice and deference require. This difficulty points once again to the need for intellectually rigorous and erudite theological education.

Truth and Tradition

AGENDA PRIORITIES

In theological education today, at least within the United Methodist system, there is little disagreement about the things that need to be taken into account somehow and somewhere. This is true for both faculties and students, and also for denominational representatives who come forward to address the seminary situation. Everyone agrees that the situation of women needs drastic improvement and will require a pervasive rethinking and then restructuring of Christian institutions. Everyone agrees that people victimized by bigotry because they are different from some majority need to be befriended, treated in neighborly fashion, and invited into full participation in the Christian community. Everyone agrees that people in countries and social strata that have not heard the Christian gospel need to be addressed in ways sensitive to their situations. Everyone agrees that contemporary expressions of the Christian interpretation of life need to be developed for the enrichment, criticism, and potential conversion of secular and other world cultures. Everyone agrees that Christian institutions need to be reevaluated and assessed according to the needs of the gospel's mission today. Everyone agrees that Christians should be committed to social justice and environmental respect and that these obligations merit the resources of the church.

But few people agree about the priorities of these items. For North American white middle-class women, the feminist agenda for the advancement of women generally is at the top of the list. For African American women, that agenda is altered by Womanist concerns also to be supportive of African American men against the vicissitudes of racial prejudice and antitraditions of hopelessness and downward inertia. For Africans in American seminaries, the oppression of middle-class white women who are paid less than their male counterparts is appreciated abstractly,

Truth and Tradition

but the top of their agenda is preoccupied with questions of the polygamous African family, the economic role of women, and the legitimacy of honoring ancestors. Recognition of same-sex unions is of utmost importance for people whose own lives must be publicly denied if they embrace that lifestyle, but this is of a much lower order of concern for those whose public success does not depend on changing current attitudes. Minorities from the inner city take urban ministry to be the top priority, whereas rural people often take the very existence of the inner city to be a distraction of attention and a moral offense to their own needs. Every racial, sexual, handicapped, subcultural, or national minority group takes the advocacy of justice for its cause to be at the top of the agenda.

So it is also with those concerned to devise a public theological expression: nothing could be more important than articulating the Christian worldview in ways that significantly address the contemporary world. On the other hand, what greater need has the church than to look at its own institutions with a prophetic eye? And how can anyone say that the causes of justice, peace, and ecological sanity should take second place to concerns about religious institutions and messages?

The items on the agenda of thinking Christians today are pretty much the same. The priority order is a source of radical controversy and division. These conflicts are felt throughout the church. The intensity of the conflicts has given rise to self-conscious countermovements, such as the "Good News" organization in The United Methodist Church whose publication published Professor Oden's popular article mentioned above. But little serious theological unity obtains within the countermovements. The hyperintellectualism of Professor Oden's cry to return to the creeds and the definition of heresy is not at all compatible with other emphases of the Good News movement on cultural conformity to Southern middle-class virtues

Truth and Tradition

[handwritten margin note: → Good News anti-intellectual!? Perhaps---]

and anti-intellectual celebration of remembered religious enthusiasms. The countermovements are expressions of anxiety about the intensity of conflict over agenda priorities among the faithful. Intensity of conflict promotes succumbing to the temptations of simplicity or authoritarianism. Yet these conflicts are at the very heart of a gospel that is supposed to be carried in appropriate, truth-bearing form to *all people* of *all nations*.

The conflicts are most succinctly focused in seminaries, for good reason. As schools, seminaries are something like play acting for real life, where you can say and do things that don't really count in order to find out what happens. On the other hand, seminaries are laboratories where the best minds, making the best arguments for their priorities, get to stake their claims and fight it out. Seminary deans and presidents like to point to the intellectual quality and commitment of their faculties as expressed in learned debates about legitimate issues of priorities in presenting the gospel. Good seminaries, however, attract good students who are the leaders-in-the-making of their communities and who present the conflicts among priorities in the theological agenda in the most pressing and practical ways. The good students demand the deepest understanding of their traditions, the most acute analyses of their situation, and the most imaginative and critically responsive interpretations of the Christian truth. Smart students know they will have to begin their ministry with what they are given in seminary, and they demand to get the most when they are paying only tuition, before they have to learn by paying with their own failures in ministry.

The obligation therefore falls upon seminaries not only to keep minimal harmony among the competing agendas but also to equip each set of legitimate priorities with viable traditions for its mission. Women's agendas need to have access to suppressed parts of the dominant European traditions in which women's roles might be found, and

56

Truth and Tradition

[margin note: Neville speaks of "traditions of ethics & natural philosophy". Are these "traditions" in the sense Hooker used the word?]

they need to appropriate traditions in modes that allow for suppression of some elements, supplementation of others, and invention of new elements. The agendas of groups victimized by bigotry need those aspects of the traditions that express neighborliness to alien kinds of people and that express condemnation of self-serving identifications of God's beloved. People for whose cultures Christianity is a novelty need access to all those traditions of radical extension and revision of traditional cultures that have characterized the Christian movement, beginning with Paul's attempt to make sense of a rural Galilean rabbi to an urban Hellenistic world. People concerned to address the Christian message to the world need access to the traditions of Christian apologetics, from Luke-Acts to St. Thomas Aquinas's *Summa contra Gentiles* to Paul Tillich's *Systemtaic Theology* and Raimundo Panikkar's *Unknown Christ of Hinduism*. Persons concerned with the structures of the church need the traditions of critical ecclesiology. Those concerned with social justice and the environment need the traditions of ethics and natural philosophy.

None of these traditions or aspects of traditions stands alone; each needs the others. Yet for different priorities, the different approaches to traditions have differential value. Who keeps all these legitimate concerns in balance and maintains the critical, self-correcting dialogue? The right answer, of course, is the church as a whole and working through the executive agency of the bishops and other high leaders. But the church rarely operates as a whole and the bishops and high leaders often are forced to exhaust themselves in more immediate causes, usually one agenda's priorities over the others. The practical answer is that the seminaries are the arena in which the balance of priorities is maintained and the diverse approaches to traditions legitimated. The seminaries are indeed the laboratories for church leadership. They ought

Truth and Tradition

to be the repository of knowledge and understanding so that ignorance and innocence are not allowed to pass. To be faithful to the traditions of the church, and effective in translating Christ's truth for the conditions of theological students, seminaries require the most severe and demanding academic standards coupled with an unflagging commitment to state the truth for our time. What a blessing to know that when you have exhausted your heart, mind, will, and strength, the divine spirit will purge your dross and turn the rest to gold. Seminaries do not deserve grief but help and a chorus of "Stand By Me."

Notes

1. Thomas C. Oden, "Confessions of a Grieving Seminary Professor," *Good News* (January/February 1994): 10-13.
2. For a different approach, see Robert C. Neville's *Highroad around Modernism* (Albany: State University of New York Press, 1992).
3. Thomas C. Oden, *The Living God: Systematic Theology: Volume One* (San Francisco: Harper & Row, 1987).
4. For a recent comprehensive biography, see Henry Rack, *Reasonable Enthusiast: John Wesley and the Rise of Methodism*, 2nd edition (Nashville: Abingdon Press, 1992).

Chapter Three

Leaders and Servants

Lovett H. Weems, Jr.

Within the people of God, there are those called to the representative ministry—ordained and diaconal. Such callings are evidenced by special gifts, evidence of God's grace, and promise of usefulness. God's call to the representative ministry is inward as it comes to the individual, and outward through the judgment and validation of the church.

The Book of Discipline, ¶108

Years ago John R. Mott said, "It is evident that no society . . . can hold together and can realize great objects without thoroughly qualified leaders. The Church of Christ is no exception. Wherever the Church has proved inadequate it has been due to inadequate leadership."[1] More recently the scholar James MacGregor Burns has said of American society, "One of the most universal cravings in our time is a hunger for compelling and creative leadership." In our time, if the church is going to be adequate to its calling, it must require thoroughly qualified, compelling, and creative leadership.

Leadership is difficult to define, but it is almost universally recognized. Bishop Rueben P. Job is right: "Ask any local congregation and they will tell you when they see it and when they don't." Leadership is not administration or management, though both of these are essential to good leadership. Rather, leadership is essentially a moral act. It is the development and articulation of a shared vision—a vision for the church and the world far different from the current reality. Leadership is about change. For Christians, the way things are is never synonymous with God's ultimate will.

To give this kind of leadership, those who enter ordained or consecrated ministry[2] must understand that ministry is a way of life, not simply a profession; that ministry is a calling, not a career. In contrast to a success culture and a maintenance church, we must hold up a model of leadership in service to a great vision. As Dean Judith Orr of Saint Paul School of Theology puts it, "Our calling is not to survive nor to succeed but to serve." Historically, those called to leadership in the church have sometimes been known as "servants of the servants of God."

THE NEED FOR ENLISTMENT

It is easy for us as United Methodists to take for granted the presence of an educated church leadership. This has not always been the case. A college may have been established at the Christmas Conference in 1784, but it was fifty years before a theological school was begun. Today the church faces a new challenge. As our need for more compelling and creative leadership grows, our church is seeing fewer persons enter professional ministry. It is also in danger of not having the quality of leadership it requires.

We believe God is always calling persons to ordained and consecrated ministry. However, all of us in the church are recognizing in a new way the need to work together to

Leaders and Servants

encourage and support persons in hearing and responding to this call.[3]

A part of our current concern for enlisting new leaders for the church comes simply from statistics. For example, the age trends among United Methodist clergy show that in 1973 21.2 percent of United Methodist clergy were under the age of 35; whereas in 1988 that percentage had dropped to 9.7 percent. You may also be familiar with the statistics of upcoming retirements. Retirements over the coming years will often be twice as high as in years just past.

Some other statistics provided by the Division of Ordained Ministry are revealing:

Average age at retirement: In 1968 it was 68; in 1992 it was 63.
Average age of seminarians: In 1968 it was 25; in 1992 it was 35.
Average expected years of service for new clergy: In 1968 it was 42 years; in 1992 it was 23 years.

There is a concern as to whether we have enough new clergy to serve the church in the coming years.

A concern for greater numbers is related to and complicated by our commitment to quality leadership for the church. Has there been a shift in who responds and who does not? Studies indicate that the answer is yes. Ronald F. Thiemann, dean of Harvard Divinity School, reports on a study conducted by the American Medical Association in 1851. They recorded the careers chosen by 12,400 men who graduated from eight leading colleges between 1800 and 1850. The largest group, 26 percent, went into ordained ministry, followed by 25 percent who went into law, and 8 percent who became physicians.[4] If such a survey of comparable colleges were done today, ministry

> The best young leaders not becoming clergy.

Truth and Tradition

would not rank high enough to be included on the statistics.

"Fewer and fewer undergraduate students who graduated at the top of their classes are coming to theological schools," observes theologian Schubert Ogden. "They are going on to other professions and careers. This is *the* problem of a church that is not reproducing the bulk of its leadership from the highest ranks of its young persons."[5]

An example of this shift came to me as I was looking through a United Methodist college yearbook from the 1950s. Page after page was like a Who's Who of The United Methodist Church. What I came to realize was that these students who entered ministry were often the outstanding students from their high schools and the outstanding leaders of a whole state. They were the people who could have pursued any endeavor and have done very well. Then, I thought about those same kinds of students today who are attending high school and college with my children and asked myself if those students are seriously considering such ministry. For the most part, they are not.

Now this does not necessarily take away from those who have responded to the call to ordained or consecrated ministry, but it does point to the many people who no longer seriously consider such ministry.

What are some of the reasons for these fewer numbers and the danger of decline in quality? The church, like many institutions in our society, is suffering from misunderstandings of leadership and, in some cases, what John Gardner calls an antileadership vaccine.

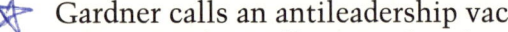

☆ We are also suffering today the effects of our church's being in decline as an organization for more than a generation. We have to remember that those young people who are not considering ordained or consecrated ministry are not refraining from doing so because of the way conference boards do their work or because of the quality of the seminary curriculum. These people never get that far. So, our efforts and our futures are tied to the renewal and revitalization of the church and its leadership. Donald H. Treese has said that, in an effort to make everything mission, we have trivialized the concept and lost the power of the mission of the church that can draw people to it like a magnet. When we trivialize what we are about, we trivialize the role of the pastor.[6]

Rebecca Chopp has said, "Ministers are weary of the caretaking and management functions that are assigned in the modern church."[7] In declining organizations, inordinate attention is given to these caretaking functions because good administration and management can give the appearance of a healthy organization for many years after the power has gone. Good caretakers will preserve the forms which developed in a previous, vital era after the power has left those forms, thus giving the illusion that everything is still the way it used to be. However, such caretaking has no power to attract the most gifted people who seek to be leaders around a new vision appropriate for a new day.

The church is also suffering today from the perception that the ministry lacks integrity. Integrity is an issue today in all professions. It is an essential element of leadership. The church—like many other institutions—has not been served well by those who have betrayed the trust of followers. What is at stake here is not the image of a profession but the ability of people to be leaders of a church. Martin Marty says that clergy often complain about living in a fishbowl: lay people are too concerned about how clergy live their lives. He says this concern is misplaced. While acknowledging that there are places where prying eyes should not go, Marty points out that clergy should become concerned primarily if lay people quit caring how they live their lives, because that will be a sure sign that they are no longer looked to as leaders.

[handwritten annotation: → leadership & integrity go together.]

Truth and Tradition

The concern for integrity simply goes with leadership. The question for a leader is always, Are you willing to wear the vision that you proclaim the way you wear clothes? Brilliance is not required for ministry, but integrity is. This credibility is won very slowly, but it can be lost very quickly, and, once lost, is exceedingly difficult to regain.

There are many facets of integrity about which all of us share a concern today, and there is a growing sense in the church that a key dimension of integrity is effectiveness. We are becoming clear that effectiveness is an ethical issue. Effectiveness is not a new issue, but it certainly has an intensity about it today that is different from some times in the past. One example came during the 1992 Episcopal Address delivered by Bishop Dale White at the General Conference. The address was interrupted many times with applause, most coming at predictable moments. Occasionally, however, spontaneous applause would erupt at places where it was not anticipated. One such time followed the sentence, "We will assist ineffective clergy to seek another vocation." Such moments tell us more than any survey can about what is troubling our church.

ENLISTMENT—OUR COMMON CALLING

Given what is troubling our church, how can we hope to enlist those whom we need for compelling and creative leadership? The responsibility for identification and enlistment for ordained and consecrated ministry is shared by many in The United Methodist Church. Laity in congregations, pastors and diaconal ministers, bishops and district superintendents, boards of ordained and diaconal ministry, and seminaries are some who share a common calling to encourage and guide those who seek to serve God in this way.

[Handwritten note at top: Fitness for ministry is the concern of the conference, not the seminary!]

Leaders and Servants

Usually in organizations, when things are not going well, different segments will tend to blame each other. Perhaps that occasionally happens to us. For example, local churches and conferences may say, "The seminaries just don't send us good enough graduates." And seminary faculty may say, "The churches don't send us good enough students."

While that blaming may occur sometimes, it does not happen often, says Candler School of Theology dean R. Kevin LaGree, because of our polity. The historic power to determine fitness for ministry has been given to the Annual Conferences. So when it comes to the enlistment, quality, preparation, and standards of ordained and consecrated ministry, we have an issue together—a common calling.

As Bishop William R. Cannon put it in speaking to the 1956 Methodist General Conference as it considered the establishment of two new seminaries: "The achievement and maintenance of a strong and sufficient ministry is the responsibility, not of a board or an agency or a school, but of the whole Church. In the end our ministry will be as numerous or as scarce, as educated or as ignorant, as strong or as weak, as good or as bad as we as a church enable it to be."

The essential mutuality of the task was captured by Leander Keck in his 1992 Lyman Beecher Lectures: "Just as seminaries will not prosper with closer supervision by unrenewed churches, so the renewal of the churches will not be advanced by seminaries in which theological scholarship . . . ignores the needs of the churches."[8]

We are all partners in this great task. While each of us will have particular roles and assignments, in the final analysis we cannot achieve what is needed by the church without working together. These are indeed good days to talk about collaborative efforts because of the openness of denominational, local church, and seminary leaders to

Truth and Tradition

cooperation around enlistment for ministry, as well as other major issues facing our denomination.
Who are those we *are* enlisting now?

SOME TRENDS

Some major changes in seminary enrollments in recent years reflect greater diversity of age, gender, and racial/ethnic groups. These changes are not peculiar to those entering religious professions.

Joseph P. O'Neill and Jerilee Grandy point out, for instance, that over the past generation an increasing proportion of women has been entering the secular professions, as well. The following chart shows the changing student breakdowns with regard to gender for medical and law schools, as well as the theological schools of the United States and Canada, representing many denominations.

	1976-77		1988-89	
	Male	Female	Male	Female
Medicine	45,145	12,940 (22.3%)	67,934	49,614 (42.2%)
Law	88,647	30,902 (25.8%)	42,576	22,854 (34.9%)
Theology	22,256	2,905 (11.5%)	20,013	6,131 (23.0%)

(Source: National Center for Education Statistics, 1992)

The enrollment of women in United Methodist seminaries is significantly higher than in theological schools as a whole because some denominations do not permit the ordination of women. Currently, women make up approximately 45 percent of the students at United Methodist seminaries seeking the Master of Divinity degree, which leads to ordination.

Leaders and Servants

O'Neill and Grandy also point out that young Americans, both women and men, have been making life choices somewhat later than they once did. For example, the median age of men entering their first marriage rose from 22.8 years of age in 1950 to 26.1 in 1990. Finishing college in four years is no longer the norm.[9]

The median age of students at United Methodist seminaries is thirty-five. Most seminaries have some very young students directly out of college, others who have delayed vocational decisions or graduate study for a few years after college, and students over thirty often referred to as "second-career" students, though this term does not fit all of them precisely. While the younger students bring immediate academic experience, the older seminarians bring rich life experience and normally have had extensive leadership experience in the local church. Each learns from the other and shares a deep appreciation for the gifts of one another.

The need for a more broadly representative leadership for the church has led to greater racial and ethnic variety in the student population of United Methodist seminaries. Today just over 14 percent of the students at United Methodist seminaries are of racial and ethnic groups other than Caucasian. The need for such diversity is highlighted by the observation that "next to the continuing movement of the baby boom generation through the life cycle, the increasing racial/ethnic diversity of the United States will be the major demographic trend through at least the first quarter of the new century."[10]

In addition, there is a greater presence on seminary campuses of students from outside the United States and from numerous language and cultural backgrounds. One reason is a desire by seminaries to function with a more global and less parochial approach. Another reason is the fast growth of immigrant congregations in the United States and their need for indigenous, trained leadership.

Truth and Tradition

One striking example is the fast growth of United Methodist congregations among Korean Americans and their expanding need for leadership.

YOUNGER STUDENTS

The increasing average age of United Methodist clergy and the declining numbers of young seminarians have led to renewed denominational efforts to lift up the call to full-time ministry for the young.

The Lilly Enlistment Project of a few years ago, sponsored by the Division of Ordained Ministry, the thirteen United Methodist seminaries, and the Lilly Endowment, was an important first step for us as a denomination in reclaiming the task of enlistment of youth. One of the efforts made possible by this project was the first national enlistment event in a generation for young people interested in ordained ministry. In many ways this event illustrates why such efforts are so important. One young person who attended was last year's student council president at Saint Paul School of Theology. A pastor who served on the design team for the event, after seeing so many excited young people there, wondered if there might be such youth in his own local church. When he went back home, he went individually to two youth leaders in his church and asked them if they had ever thought about ordained ministry. To his surprise, each of them said, "Yes, I have." This pastor asked himself, "How many other young people like these two have there been in my churches over the past thirty years who needed me to encourage them?" The overwhelming response to this first national event (more youth wanted to attend than could) led to follow-up consultations which have been held twice since at two-year intervals.

Leaders and Servants

A study of youth likely to enter seminary found that they are those who participate in religious activities in high school and college. These students also tend to be more altruistic, more socially involved, and academically more able than students who do not participate in religious activities. Their attitudes toward financial well-being and worldly success are sharply different from the vast majority of their college-going peers.[11]

O'Neill and Grandy also found that, even when entrance into an occupation is postponed, the last two years of high school and the early years of college continue to be an important time for making lasting career decisions. For example, almost two-thirds of the men and almost half of the women first-year seminarians they surveyed in 1992 and 1993 said they had first considered a religious profession in their high school or college years.[12]

Perhaps we should all remember the words of a seminary president who said in 1905 that the principal reason why young people "of the highest qualifications are not entering the ministry in larger numbers is the lack of definite, earnest, prayerful efforts to influence them to devote themselves to this calling."[13]

What kind of ongoing preparation and support is needed by these future leaders? One responsibility is to prepare these future leaders in a way that includes their identity as United Methodist leaders. Perhaps the best way to develop that identity is to encourage prospective seminary students to consider attendance at a United Methodist seminary.

UNITED METHODIST SEMINARIES

The United Methodist Church is served by those who have gone to various United Methodist seminaries, as well as persons who have gone to other seminaries. Many

Truth and Tradition

church members have raised concerns about the large number of United Methodist seminarians who attend non–United Methodist seminaries. There are a number of understandable reasons for this happening. Some of these include:

- *United Methodist policy.* We are one of the few denominations that has a relatively laissez-faire policy about where our students go. This approach has changed for many denominations in recent years but not for The United Methodist Church. While seminaries must be approved by the University Senate, there is no requirement, as some denominations now have, to attend a denominational seminary for at least a portion of a student's theological education. Last year United Methodist students were enrolled in 127 different seminaries.
- *Regional trends.* In the last twenty years students have been going to seminaries closer to home. Today, for United Methodist seminarians, geography and denomination are of equal importance as factors in choosing a seminary. Students are often more likely to attend a seminary nearer to them, even if it is of a denomination other than their own.
- *Cost.* Many non–United Methodist seminaries are far less expensive. Economic considerations have taken on greater significance as the average age and average educational indebtedness per student have gone up.
- *Student appointments.* Related to the cost issue is the availability of student appointments where a non–United Methodist seminary is located. In fact, some students report that they are encouraged to take, or continue, such student appointments rather than relocate to United Methodist seminaries.
- *Theological positions.* Surveys show that for those attending non–United Methodist seminaries, theological

we need to ground students in the Wesleyan ethos ★

position is more important than for United Methodist seminarians as a whole. This appears to account for the fact that a number of United Methodist seminarians attend non–United Methodist seminaries associated with a distinct theological position.

The primary concern that arises from these facts is the issue of denominational identity. One reason for this concern is that, of the United Methodist seminarians who attend non–United Methodist seminaries, one-half did not grow up in The United Methodist Church. In these cases, more is needed than courses of history, doctrine, and polity. These students need to be a part of the ethos, worship, and daily conversations about issues that go on at United Methodist seminaries.

One way for The United Methodist Church to renew itself in the spirit and tradition of its Wesleyan heritage is to prepare leaders deeply grounded in that heritage through our United Methodist seminaries.

FUNDING

Another dimension of preparation and support for future leaders is finance. The basic funding source for the education of these leaders for The United Methodist Church is the Ministerial Education Fund (MEF). The MEF began in the Southeastern Jurisdiction and the South Central Jurisdiction as the Two Percent Fund. The philosophy was that 2 percent of church expenditures would be set aside for the education of seminarians. This plan and formula were adopted by The United Methodist Church in 1968 as the national funding method for our seminaries. The genius was in the formula. It assumed that money for future leadership would rise or fall with overall church expenditures. Everything went well until

Truth and Tradition

local church expenditures started growing so rapidly that there was a desire to change the formula. The 2 percent was kept, but the base on which the 2 percent was figured was changed. In fact, for several quadrennia the original formula has been changed so as to produce a predetermined figure rather than staying with the genius of the original concept. The effects of these actions have been devastating.

What has been happening in recent years fits a longer historical pattern of decline in support of training for future pastoral leadership. For example, in the 1930s denominations paid 90 percent of the cost of educating their future pastors. In 1968, when the MEF came in, this figure for The United Methodist Church was 32 percent. This percentage remained stable until the formula began to be altered, and then a dramatic decline set it. By 1989, the MEF contributed only 20 percent toward the cost of educating each student. By 1990 it had dropped to 19 percent, by 1991 to 18 percent, and by 1993 to 17 percent. It appears that this percentage will continue to drop over the coming years.

This declining percentage is not the result of increased spending by the seminaries. In fact, over the last ten years, United Methodist seminaries have had budget increases of 2 percent a year less than the budget increases of all seminaries of all denominations.

As the portion of the cost of educating each student paid by the denomination decreases, tuition must increase. This is true despite the heroic efforts of all the seminaries in financial development. The increase in tuition is now reflected in the growing educational indebtedness of seminarians, which is such a concern to all of us. To put it quite frankly, the church is making entrepreneurs out of seminary leaders and debtors out of students.

If we, together, cannot turn around this trend toward shifting the cost from denomination to student, then the future will not be bright for seminaries or our students. It

Leaders and Servants

is a critical time. We may reach a point in the not too distant future when we will not be able to brag about having perhaps the finest family of theological schools in the nation. If that becomes the case, it will be because of some very shortsighted financial decisions.

WHAT'S AT STAKE?

As Bishop Ann B. Sherer has said, "There is a fundamental right to leadership in the church." What is the calling of the United Methodist seminaries? At the most important level we are about the very future of the church and developing the leadership that the church deserves.

Our futures, those of local United Methodist churches and United Methodist seminaries, are bound together. United Methodist churches cannot be strong without vital United Methodist seminaries. Likewise, we in the thirteen United Methodist seminaries cannot do our work well without close and ongoing interaction with those in the churches who brought us into being, who have supported us through the years, and for whom we are preparing a new generation of leaders in the Wesleyan tradition.

There is no more important task before Christians today than the enlistment and education of leaders for the church. The future of the church depends upon our ability to enlist and prepare committed and capable candidates for ministry. In the coming years, a high percentage of current United Methodist pastors must be replaced. Even more important than the number is the church's need for pastors and diaconal ministers with outstanding gifts and graces to meet the challenges of today and tomorrow.

No educational institutions in the world will have more impact on the future of United Methodist churches than United Methodist seminaries. There is no way for local churches and The United Methodist Church finally

Truth and Tradition

to accomplish our goals without a strong and vital denominational family of theological schools. As a leading student of the history of theological education in this country, Dr. Robert W. Lynn, has put it: "Make no mistake about it. What happens today in the theological schools will affect the church for decades to come. As the seminary goes, so goes American Protestantism."

Conclusion

Ordained and consecrated ministry are perhaps the most challenging and demanding of all vocations. They are also the most rewarding and fulfilling. When done poorly, such ministry is a disgrace. When done well, there is nothing more wonderful to behold. Indeed, there is no higher calling. There is no greater responsibility than to be involved as we all can be in the enlistment, encouragement, education, guidance, and approval of persons seeking to give their lives to God through ordained and consecrated ministry.

We in the thirteen United Methodist seminaries seek always to do our work in such a way as to merit the confidence placed in us by the church. We do that through the depth of our faith and commitment to Jesus Christ, through the quality of the teaching and learning that takes place, and especially through the effectiveness of our graduates in ministry.

For fifty years, up and down and across all of England, through forty thousand sermons, John Wesley kindled and nurtured what we now know as the Wesleyan Revival. At the heart of that movement of God was a theological affirmation, a message. John Wesley felt that it was a particular message from God that he was called to deliver and share with others. Events have borne out the fact that this was a significant movement in the history of the Christian faith—a moment when message and leadership

Leaders and Servants

were grafted together. Although many factors influenced the success of the Wesleyan movement, we must always remember that it flourished because of the clear and challenging message it proclaimed and the energetic leadership provided by John Wesley.

We in the United Methodist seminaries are educating a new generation of leaders in the Wesleyan tradition. And, given the needs both of the world and the church, this new generation of "circuit riders" will be called upon to out-preach, out-pray, out-love, out-study, and, finally, out-endure all of us who have served before. That is a monumental mandate, but nothing less will do for those called of God to ministry.

NOTES

1. John R. Mott, *The Future Leadership of the Church* (New York: YMCA, 1980), 4.
2. In The United Methodist Church, clergy are ordained and diaconal ministers are consecrated.
3. A resource designed for those considering ordained and consecrated ministry is *The Christian as Minister*, available from Cokesbury. A superb volume to offer anyone considering ordained ministry is Dennis M. Campbell, *Who Will Go for Us?* (Nashville: Abingdon Press, 1994).
4. Ronald F. Thiemann, "Toward the Integrated Study of Religion," *Harvard Divinity Bulletin* 21:4 (1992): 15.
5. *Perspective*, Perkins School of Theology (Winter, 1993): 11-12.
6. Donald H. Treese, "Reaffirming the Covenant in Itinerary," in *Send Me?* ed. Donald E. Messer (Nashville: Abingdon Press, 1991), 77.
7. Rebecca S. Chopp, "Liberation for a Culture in Crisis," in Messer, *Send Me?* 154.
8. Leander E. Keck, *The Church Confident* (Nashville: Abingdon Press, 1993), 120.
9. Joseph P. O'Neill and Jerilee Grandy, "The Image of Ministry: Attitudes of Young Adults Toward Organized Religion and Religious Professions," *Ministry Research Notes* (Princeton, N.J.: Educational Testing Service, Summer, 1994), 2.
10. David A. Roozen and C. Kirk Hadaway, "Individuals and the Church Choice," in *Church and Denominational Growth*, ed. David A. Roozen and C. Kirk Hadaway (Nashville: Abingdon Press, 1993), 249.
11. O'Neill and Grandy, "The Image of Ministry," 18.
12. Ibid., 3.
13. W. W. Moore, Inaugural Address, Union Theological Seminary, Richmond, Vir., May 9, 1905.

Chapter Four

Freedom and Accountability

Judith E. Smith

For more than 150 years, the church has argued about the education of its clergy. This discussion has taken place in every arena in the church. Clergy and laity alike have voiced strong opinions. In the mid-nineteenth century the argument focused around whether it was wise to even allow present and future preachers to attend a theological school. A hundred years later the arguments revolved around whether or not a seminary education would become the norm in our denomination. And at the 1992 General Conference, heated discussion occurred about whether the 1952 decision to make seminary education the norm should be revised with a return to the Course of Study as an equal route to ordained ministry.

In all of these discussions, the question has remained the same: How does the church best equip those persons who are called by God to serve the church of Jesus Christ in its ministry in and to the world? Over time, of course, the nature of congregations and the role of the clergy have changed, and the nuances of the arguments have shifted. In the nineteenth century, much of the push for seminary education came because educated laity no longer wanted to hear uneducated preachers. In addition, denominations that provided the possibility of seminary education were attracting some of Methodism's brightest prospects. On the other side of the argument were those who were fearful that a formal education would have a negative effect on the evangelistic zeal and personal piety of the preachers. Those who won the day insisted that study and the practice of piety would not be separated but could be united in the educational process.

WHO OWNS THE SEMINARIES?

All of those concerns sound very familiar. When the church had no seminaries and was considering whether or not to establish them, the primary question was one of control. Who would own these seminaries? When the Course of Study was the only form of pastoral education available, competing concerns were just as clearly articulated. Voices of various theological persuasion regularly advocated their own particular perspective. Today the question remains the same. How does the church best equip those persons who are called by God to serve the church of Jesus Christ in its ministry in and to the world? Who determines the shape and content of theological education? In other words, Who owns the seminaries? These questions are probably more intense during a time of rapid change, such as we now face. The church is living in an "in-between time," a time when almost everyone is talking about "changing paradigms" and looking for new—and positive—language to describe the "mainline churches" which no longer seem so mainline. We have watched our membership decline and we are currently discussing options for restructuring the denomination. And most of all, we are seeking to understand our mission in this changing world.

The seminaries face the same changes that are facing the society in which they operate. This is a time of economic change when resources seem to be more scarce.

Truth and Tradition

Local congregations find their financial resources eaten up by the cost of pensions and health insurance for their clergy; so, many of them are reducing those expenditures over which they do have control. Consequently, the church's support for its seminaries has been declining. The seminaries, which face the same economic issues that the local churches are facing, find that the cost of theological education rises relentlessly year after year. In spite of the increased dollar amount allocated for the seminaries by the denomination each year, the percentage of their budgets that it underwrites has decreased consistently over the last twenty years. In 1972 the Ministerial Education Fund, most of which helps to underwrite seminary education, made up approximately 33 percent of the operating budgets of the thirteen United Methodist seminaries. In 1992 it provided less than 20 percent of those budgets. During the same period of time, student tuition has moved in exactly the opposite direction, so that on a line graph the two sources of income form an almost perfect X, with the MEF dropping from over 30 percent to less than 20 percent and tuition dollars increasing from less than 20 percent to more than 30 percent. With each passing year the seminaries have to search for new sources of funding to underwrite their operations or face raising tuition to an unacceptable level. More and more money must come from sources outside the structures of The United Methodist Church. Who, then, owns the seminaries?

The seminaries also face the same changing demographics that confront our entire culture. People are living longer, marrying later, raising children in single-parent families, and changing careers at least once and sometimes two or three times. Women are finding their place in traditionally male professions and racial/ethnic diversity is increasing in every geographic area across the country. Local congregations find that their members no longer have the kind of denominational loyalty that once existed.

Freedom and Accountability

Many of them have no background or experience in a United Methodist congregation—or perhaps in any congregation. They come with little biblical or historical knowledge and they move from denomination to denomination when they change neighborhoods and communities. They are interested not in denominational identity but in the shape of the local church.

Our seminary students come from the laity in our congregations. Many of them are second-career students who find it difficult to pack up and move across the country to attend "the seminary of their choice." They must consider families who are settled, and they often need to maintain current employment to help with the cost of their education. Loyalty to The United Methodist Church will no longer guarantee an adequate number of students any more than it will guarantee an adequate number of dollars. And so seminaries are asking themselves what it takes to attract the students without which the school cannot exist. Accommodation must happen on both sides of the equation. The shape of seminary communities, which is a vital part of theological education, has changed to respond to commuter students, families, and part-time students. How is the seminary to decide when there is too much accommodation and when there is too little? How can they respond to the needs of a changing culture without compromising too drastically the unique nature of theological education? After all, who owns the seminaries?

All of these factors have an impact on the seminaries and confuse the issue of ownership. In addition to the economic and demographic factors, the seminary must deal with competing claims from accrediting bodies. The United Methodist seminaries relate to the University Senate, the Theological Education Commission, the Association of United Methodist Theological Schools, and the Association of Theological Schools. In addition, each

Truth and Tradition

one relates to regional secular accrediting bodies. The theological school must balance the claims of these groups for academic excellence with the sometimes competing claims of local congregations and the larger church. Who does own the seminaries?

The denomination also makes claims on the seminaries through boards of ordained and diaconal ministry which award credentials to their graduates and bishops and cabinets who appoint them to serve. Their concerns about the quality of education that prospective clergy and diaconal ministers receive give them a significant stake in the shape of theological education. Each year they interview seminary students seeking ordination, consecration, and appointment. They listen from the perspective of the local churches in which they live and work, and they evaluate the potential effectiveness of the candidates. The theological schools will send their students before these annual conference boards, and so they know that they must take very seriously conference claims on the institution. Who owns the seminaries?

An increasing number of caucuses and other special interest groups in the church also make claims upon the seminaries. Widely divergent groups in The United Methodist Church want the seminaries to take seriously the needs of their constituents. Some of these groups are articulating the changing conditions in the culture and calling for the schools to pay attention, such as those concerned about race and gender issues. Others are committed to particular programmatic emphases in local congregations and want the seminaries to teach courses that will enable pastors to be more effective in those areas. Some of these groups are official bodies of the denomination with formal claims on the seminaries. Others do not have institutional power but raise compelling questions about preparation for effective ministry in local congregations. The theological schools must constantly seek a

Freedom and Accountability

balance in evaluating and responding faithfully rather than uncritically to the judgments from these church bodies. So who does own the seminaries?

And then there are more than 35,000 local congregations. Across The United Methodist Church discussions about "clergy effectiveness" are occurring in congregations of every shape and size and among those responsible for ordaining and appointing pastors and diaconal ministers to those congregations. The conversations are prompted by complaints about incompetent leaders, competing understandings of effectiveness, critical issues of low morale, and research indicating that a shortage of clergy is almost upon us. Many who are concerned about the competency and effectiveness of clergy tend to place blame on the seminary. Annual conferences and local congregations want the theological schools to guarantee that their graduates will be effective pastors and congregational leaders. Too often they believe that the whole responsibility for effectiveness lies with the seminary. If the seminary would only teach more courses or different courses or teach them differently, the students would be more effective pastors. When churches struggle to cope with ineffective leadership they raise the question most loudly of all: Who owns the seminaries?

When each of these parties raises the question, the implication is that if they were the real owners, the results would be better. When we look at it from that perspective, ownership is tied most closely to control. Who is it that controls what goes on in the seminaries? Who determines what is taught? Who decides which students will attend? Who influences the shape of the community? When the voices find themselves in competition with one another, each one seeks to have the greatest influence on the outcome. And when they are confronted with the reality that in three years' time the seminaries cannot do all that they want, the tensions become even greater.

Truth and Tradition

Freedom and Accountability

It is easy to believe that the tensions would disappear if only we could find the right answer to the ownership question. The truth is that the tensions have been there since the beginning. Various voices have asserted their convictions about the best way to equip those persons who are called by God to serve the church of Jesus Christ in its ministry in and to the world. In the midst of even the most heated discussions we have affirmed the belief that these tensions should not only be tolerated but embraced. Both the seminaries and the church have argued for a balance between freedom and accountability. Gerald McCulloh, in his book *Ministerial Education in the American Methodist Movement*, argued that the best interests of both the church and the school are served by "a trustful independence as well as responsible interdependence. . . . The churches and the schools must be free, on occasions and on issues, to say yes or no to each other."[1]

Until the early twentieth century, Methodist Episcopal bishops had the power to confirm faculty appointments at all seminaries. In 1905 they refused to confirm the election of Hinckley Mitchell to the faculty of Boston University School of Theology for theological reasons. In 1908 the General Conference removed from the bishops the power to confirm faculty. Since that time no doctrinal control has been imposed on the theological schools by the denomination. Instead, the church consistently has affirmed its commitment that freedom and accountability are to be held in constant tension as a way of supporting and undergirding the search for truth. "As Schubert Ogden put it, 'the existence of radical theological freedom in the church is the clearest evidence it can give of its deep conviction in the abiding truth of its witness.'"[2]

In the face of rapid change in the church and culture, including our declining membership and influence, those

Freedom and Accountability

voices that call for doctrinal control of the seminaries by the denomination often become louder. Those same conservative and liberal voices that speak in other arenas of our common life also speak in this arena. It is just as difficult for the seminaries as it is for the larger church to respond appropriately to these voices in ways that support our vision of unity and diversity. The seminaries must be free to explore constantly the content of the Christian faith and to test various understandings in light of our knowledge and our experience. To compromise that freedom is to undercut the search for God's truth: this freedom on the part of the theological schools is as important to the church as it is to the schools themselves. The seminaries, by their very nature, can focus more time and energy than most of us can reflecting on the meaning of God's Word and the traditions of the church for this current generation. Their great contribution to the intellectual life of the church is to educate future leaders who can serve the church out of an open and seeking stance, preaching and witnessing to their faith in Jesus Christ in this generation of change and confusion. Subsequently, laity throughout the denomination will come to understand their own call to live faithfully in the world.

Issues surrounding the diversity of the community of faith are also directly related to issues of freedom and accountability in the seminaries. If the church is to live out the inclusiveness of God's reign on earth, then both the church and the theological schools must listen to widely diverse voices within the community of faith. Again the seminary has a distinctive role to play in supporting the radical inclusivity of the Body of Christ. Here a variety of voices can be heard without threat, and various theological and cultural perspectives can be presented and considered. Not all perspectives will be embraced; nor is the seminary required to agree with all theological perspectives, but all will be attended to and explored in

Truth and Tradition

respectful and responsible ways. To be faithful to our calling we must pay attention to those on the margins whose voices are often silenced by the larger and louder majority. The seminaries provide one of the places where those voices can be heard and tested in an arena where various theological perspectives are respected.

CONTROL OR INVESTMENT?

If we are to assert, then, that the tensions will always be present and, in fact, healthy, then perhaps the need, in these changing times, is to reinterpret the question "Who owns the seminaries?" Most commonly we understand that question as a question about control. The owners are those who have the most control over the seminaries. The perceived need for control is heightened in a time of rapid change and confusion, especially when the change is one of decline. But there is another way of understanding the question. When we think about the possibility of owning a piece of property, we do not first think about how much control we will have over that property. Instead, our first question is about how much we will have to invest in order to own the property. Perhaps we need to understand the question about our seminaries in the same way. Instead of looking at the amount of control as the measure of ownership, it would be more in keeping with our understanding of faithfulness to the gospel to look at who is investing the most as the measure of ownership. Then each competing voice, in order to increase its ownership of theological education in this denomination, would seek to increase its investment rather than to increase its control. While an increase in financial investment would certainly be welcomed by all of the institutions, each of the various constituencies has other, equally critical, ways of investing itself in the seminaries. Over the years those

Freedom and Accountability

levels of investment have changed, contributing to the current issues facing theological schools.

One of the most obvious ways of investing in theological seminaries is by sending them students. Local congregations can involve themselves in that effort from the time an individual seeks to discern God's call until he or she is through seminary and serving a congregation. One of the changes in recent years is a decline in the involvement of congregations in articulating God's call to others. Some of the traditional ways of doing that, such as youth camps and vocational events, are less prominent in the program life of the church. Local churches have an opportunity to invest themselves in theological education by renewing their commitment to articulate the possibility of God's call to members of their own congregation, both youth and persons in midcareer. This increased investment in nurturing leaders might well result in an increased financial investment on the part of the local church, not only in congregational support of the Ministerial Education Fund but also in additional support of individual students from that local church. More important, it would result in an increased investment in time and emotional energy on the part of the membership.

Until 1940 it was the responsibility of the local church to license pastors. The normative way to enter the ordained ministry was not to attend a theological school but to take the Course of Study. In fact, an individual who chose to attend seminary was also required to complete the Course of Study. Not until 1952 did a seminary education become the normative route to ordained ministry. When local churches were involved in licensing, they felt a much greater responsibility to determine whether an individual would be an effective pastor. In the current candidacy process, the congregation's primary role is to give their approval to an individual who wants to become a candidate. In many congregations, the decision has more

Truth and Tradition

to do with whether or not they think that individual is a good person than whether or not he or she has the capacity for effective ministry. There is an assumption that decisions about the person's qualifications will be made by district and annual conference structures; therefore, the local church need not be too concerned about that. And indeed, the process has functioned in exactly that way, with the district committee and annual conference board taking a much stronger role in determining who will be ordained or consecrated. The result may well be a lessened investment on the part of the congregation in the theological education of that particular individual.

A related result of the changes going on in congregations is that many who feel called to representative ministry have little background in biblical studies, church history, or theology. Gone are the days when students committed themselves to ministry in time to take introductory religion courses in college. With the increase in second-career students, educational backgrounds vary even more than in previous generations. The decline in denominational loyalty means many students do not even have much personal history in the church. Local congregations who take seriously lay education could provide an arena where members of the congregation could engage in biblical and theological study and reflection that would provide some background for those intending to enter seminary as well as enhancing the life of the congregation. A seminary or college with a religion department located nearby could provide resources to help with such a program. An effort like this would develop a sense of partnership in theological education and would multiply the investment of potential students, congregations, and seminaries.

The decline in denominational loyalty has also affected the calling of persons to representative ministry in some unexpected ways. When congregations feel less connected

Freedom and Accountability

to other United Methodist congregations, the commitment to quality ministry for the whole church is lessened. Large churches have the potential to nurture and send forth a number of future leaders for the denomination. These persons may well spend their ministry serving much smaller congregations who will send forth far fewer people. Unless the larger congregations understand themselves to be closely connected with all other local churches, they will feel far less responsibility for nurturing the future ministry of the whole church.

Bishops, cabinets, and annual conference boards of ordained and diaconal ministry, as indicated earlier, have a significant stake in the shape of theological education. They listen to the voices of the congregations they serve and to the candidates for ministry who come before them. Perhaps more than any other group, these boards are concerned about the content of theological education. They are at the center of the tension over what subject areas are to be required of seminary students and their answers vary widely. In discussions of clergy effectiveness the questions of theological grounding and technical expertise live in constant tension. From the beginning of theological education in the nineteenth century this tension has existed. The advocates of seminary education did not set out to educate for a profession but to add knowledge to God's call. Since that time, the church has struggled to understand what that means. As the culture has become more complex and the tasks of ministry have expanded, the discussion has continued.

A basic seminary education still takes only three short years, and yet the church has come to expect education not only in understanding the texts and the traditions and their meaning for our time, but also in such areas as administration, sociology, pastoral care, Christian education, evangelism, history of religions, religion and art, financial management, urban and rural ministries, ethnic

Truth and Tradition

histories, and ministry with persons with handicapping conditions, to name just a few. The increasing complexity of ministry itself means that

> from ten to fourteen different disciplines, a small host of denominational requirements, and some attention to the varieties of ministerial settings must be supposedly "mastered" within three academic years. Most master's degrees focus upon a single subject area, but ministry is like an ever-diversifying vocation, requiring more and more subject areas to provide a beginning competence level.[3]

Given those current curricular demands, it is no wonder that major conversations have taken place during the last decade or more wrestling with the nature of theological education by those who teach in and administer seminaries.[4] Many of these conversations have focused on the tension between theological education as the shaping of a person's growth in his or her relationship to God, including the ability to think and act theologically, and the teaching of tasks to be carried out by practitioners of the ministerial vocation. Another way of framing the issue is to focus on the tension between the *doing of theology* and the *practice of ministry*. There are strong voices in the current discussion who assert that the two cannot be separated in the way that we have tried to do. David Kelsey has recently suggested that "the purpose of a theological school is to seek to understand God more truly, and that a school's 'nature' follows from this 'purpose.'"[5]

When we are faced with the membership decline in the denomination, the changing nature of local congregations, and shrinking financial resources, it is tempting to believe that more effective techniques are the answer. In the business world a myriad of new and more effective management techniques promises to deliver a healthier bottom line. Is the same not true in theological education? If we can identify the skills lacking in ineffective ordained and diaconal ministers, we can make certain that those skills are taught in our seminaries. This is a much more tangible way to grasp the issue than to ask for graduates who out of their own relationship with God, and through their seminary education, have developed the intellectual capacity to connect theological understandings and daily life, the ability to live and act faithfully out of those connections, and the ability to help others to do the same. In an address to the Association of United Methodist Theological Schools, President Neal F. Fisher of Garrett-Evangelical Theological Seminary said it this way:

> Interested parties will frequently urge the seminary to become more functional in its education because the lack of certain skills is perhaps more tangible and identifiable than the absence of a basic encounter with God in one's spirit, mind, and will. But the lack of the latter effectively undermines any proficiency, however polished, one may have gained in the former. That is to say that the development of a full-orbed relationship with God requires reflection, discipline, and formation, which is not easily subsumed in a list of professional skills. . . . The skills in ministry demand a person who is in mind and spirit prepared to think theologically, to reflect with the Christian community upon God's doing in the past and the divine manifestation in the present.[6]

When annual conference boards of ordained and diaconal ministry find themselves faced with evaluating the potential effectiveness of candidates for ministry and ask who owns the seminaries, perhaps their own investment might be increased by new understandings of shared responsibility for theological education. In the article cited earlier, Marjorie Suchocki has suggested some radical revisions of the process of theological education. She suggests that perhaps we might look at the three years spent

Truth and Tradition

earning an M.Div. degree as the time to master the texts and the traditions. In this way the content of the degree would focus around a core curriculum and would allow for more depth of knowledge in these areas, contributing to the student's capacity to think theologically and reflect with the community on God's activity in the world.

If this model were followed, the two years of probationary membership between the completion of the M.Div. and ordination as an elder would become the field education of the pastor. Congregations who are willing could become teaching congregations and would work with the appointed pastor as she or he sought to master the functions of ministry. An increasing number of annual conference boards of ordained ministry are already taking seriously the task of ongoing education during these probationary years. This model simply formalizes and expands the content while also extending the involvement of seminaries and congregations. In Suchocki's model, seminaries and districts would provide frequent workshops in areas such as pastoral care, administration, and education. Daily involvement in local congregations would provide a far more effective arena than the typical field education placement.[7]

Perhaps the most intriguing aspect of Suchocki's proposal is the possibility of increasing the investment of all of the "owners" of the seminaries. Local congregations would be invested not only in articulating the possibility of God's call to ministry and in taking seriously the gifts and abilities of those who come before them but in the actual process of educating the future leaders of the church. Their own role in witnessing to their faith in this time and place would take on new dimensions as they helped to shape ordained and diaconal ministers.

Conclusion

Who owns the seminaries? The question sounds quite different when all of the dialogue partners seek to invest themselves more fully in the enterprise of theological education. The balance of freedom and accountability takes on new meaning when all of those making a claim on the seminaries see themselves as participants in a mutual endeavor. What if congregations invested themselves in articulating God's call to ministry to bright and capable persons, in discerning and testing that call with the individual, and then in participating in their education? What if theological schools invested themselves in working with congregations as partners in the task of educating the future leadership of the church? What if large congregations intentionally set out to call forth, nurture, and financially support future leaders on behalf of small congregations who have fewer resources? What if the denomination invested itself in financially supporting theological schools and students in a wide variety of ways, truly believing that the future of the church depended on their efforts? What if annual conference boards of ordained and diaconal ministry invested themselves in supporting a creative and innovative process of lifelong learning for all ordained and diaconal ministers?

Of course there are congregations and students and seminaries and cabinets and boards who do invest themselves in all of these ways. But the sense of mutual responsibility is not widespread. To achieve mutual responsibility would require both a willingness to let go of the need to control the seminaries and a commitment to invest significant time and energy on the part of all who are involved. Congregations would make personal and financial sacrifices. The denomination and the annual conferences would make difficult decisions about allocation of resources. Theological schools would invite

Truth and Tradition

greater participation on the part of their partners in this effort. None of that is easy, but "the challenge of providing the church with a learned ministry is so great that the seminaries alone or the clergy alone or the congregations alone or the denominational boards alone cannot adequately address the issue; we must address it together."[8] When we have done that, even in the midst of the tensions that enrich our common life, we will know who owns the seminaries.

Notes

1. Gerald O. McCulloh, *Ministerial Education in the American Methodist Movement* (Nashville: United Methodist Board of Higher Education and Ministry, Division of Ordained Ministry, 1980), pp. 309-10.
2. Neal F. Fisher, "United Methodist Seminaries and Relationships with Other Interested Parties," *Occasional Paper*, United Methodist Board of Higher Education and Ministry, January 25, 1993; quoting Schubert Ogden "Doctrinal Standards in The United Methodist Church," in *Doctrine and Theology in The United Methodist Church*, ed. Thomas A. Langford (Nashville: Kingswood Books, 1991), 45.
3. Marjorie H. Suchocki, "A Learned Ministry?" *Quarterly Review* (Summer 1993): 5.
4. See especially Edward Farley, *Theologia* (Philadelphia: Fortress Press, 1983) and *The Fragility of Knowledge* (Philadelphia: Fortress Press, 1988); and Charles M. Wood, *Vision and Discernment* (Atlanta: Scholars Press, 1985).
5. David H. Kelsey, *To Understand God Truly* (Louisville: Westminster/John Knox, 1992), 15.
6. Fisher "United Methodist Seminaries," 7.
7. Suchocki, "Learned Ministry," 16.
8. Ibid.

Chapter Five

Congregation and Academy

*Anne Streaty Wimberly and
Edward P. Wimberly*

In recent years a repeated criticism of the theology school is that it continues to pay greater attention to the academy and wider culture than it does to the local church.[1] Many in the institutional church feel that the seminary pays far too much attention to the academy and to the world than to congregations. Those who sit in the pew and those who direct the institutional church from the top feel neglected and alienated from the seminary. Their criticism highlights the need within seminaries to engage in self-examination that entails looking at how they understand themselves and their mission. A kind of review is needed that holds potential for affirming the integrity of the claim of congregations on the activity of the theology school. Included in this is the need for seminaries to develop an ecclesiology that takes into consideration the common mission in which both seminary and church participate. This entails considering the corporate nature of the church and the overarching Story that provides the raison d'être for seminary and congregational life.

This chapter will explore a narrative paradigm as a way of forging a foundation for reconnecting the seminary and

Truth and Tradition

the local church. As part of that exploration, we will examine sources of alienation between the seminary and the church as congregation and institution and proposals to alleviate alienation. A narrative paradigm will be proposed as a foundation for reconnecting the seminary and the church. We will also consider the role of vocation in the narrative paradigm, and the formation of a common ecclesiological language in the narrative paradigm. Finally, we will suggest possible structures for developing partnerships between the seminary and the congregation.

SOURCES OF ALIENATION BETWEEN SEMINARY AND CONGREGATION AND PROPOSALS TO ALLEVIATE ALIENATION

There is some historical evidence that the alienation between the seminary and the church as congregation and institution is real. One of the reasons for the alienation has been traced to the need for academic respectability on behalf of seminary professors.[2] This need was identified in a study report of graduate education in religion made by Claude Welch in 1971. The report detailed the results of a survey of religion in North American colleges, universities, and seminaries completed in 1970. One of the conclusions of the study was that there needed to be a distinction between graduate education in seminaries and religious studies within universities. The tone of the report was that to have credibility and standing the study of religion would need to give up its ecclesiastical connections. Further, Welch felt that "most seminaries, except for those connected to well-respected universities, were either 'marginal' or 'inadequate.' ".[3]

The study left the impression that the training of ministers in theological subjects at seminaries was inferior. The result has been that the primary orientation of religious education focused on the academy or university rather than the church.[4] The need for credibility within the academy became more important to many professors in seminaries than connections with the church. Moreover, the ascendance of scientific methodological sophistication became connected to respectability in religious study. In short, the 1970 study of graduate religious education became the basis on which seminary faculties evaluated themselves during the 1970s and 1980s. The result was that ecclesiastical connections of the seminary to the church became less of a focus.

As the schism between the seminary and the church evolved, the critique was made that the seminary has become a "professional school," dominated by a clergy paradigm.[5] Central to this critique is the functionalist orientation of the paradigm evidenced by the emphasis on developing individuals to fill competently the role and functions of clergy. In this paradigm, the overarching and governing goal of theological education is to equip individuals for effective ministry practice.[6]

Joseph C. Hough, Jr., argues that the issue confronting the seminary is not associated with the "clergy paradigm." Rather, the issue has to do with "professional" images of the minister or the precise character of the minister that is formed at the theological school. Bound up with this concern is the seminary's need to see itself as a professional school focused on character formation and on cooperating with the churches to ensure the kind of character formation needed in local congregations.[7]

Another response to the clergy paradigm was James Hopewell's call for a "congregational paradigm" for theological education, which focuses on the life and development of the congregation. This paradigm calls for the seminary to probe the language of community as means of contributing to an understanding of how distinctive communities are held together and express themselves.[8]

Truth and Tradition

This paradigm prompted concern because of its potential for reductionistic thinking if the scientific method became the primary basis for congregational analysis. Moreover, concern was raised that such a model might encourage the ingrownness of the church from which it already suffers.[9]

THE NARRATIVE PARADIGM: A PROPOSAL FOR TODAY

In the late 1980s a new language emerged in the seminary that holds out hope for the reconnection of the seminary and the church. This language evolved out of narrative theology with its focus on the story of the life of people and communities in the light of the Story of God's activity and Word. Our position is that, in an important way, the language of narrative holds potential for relating aspects of the "clerical paradigm" and the "congregational paradigm" in a coherent and creative way.

The narrative paradigm in theological education is a postmodern phenomenon that recognizes a shift away from grounding religion in scientific proof and toward exploring the narrative bases of human religious behavior.[10] The narrative paradigm focuses on the connection of two facets. In one facet, this new and emerging model moves the focus away from the theory-practice and functionalist-oriented model that emphasizes credentialed knowledge and mastery of professional skills. The new model emphasizes developing spiritually mature ministers who are in touch with their own story—how it may be shaped and reshaped in light of their understanding of the Christian story—and discernment of their role as minister.

The narrative paradigm focuses on developing ministers who have a passion for living the faith and who see themselves as called to interpret their faith story in ways that help others in their ongoing spiritual life and development. The model also gives credence to developing ministers who have knowledge, professional skills, and intellectual capacity to hear and see ways distinctive communities tell about and live their stories. These skills form a basis for helping congregations to become responsive communities, whose stories exhibit the Christian story, and to reflect critically on their lived story.

The second facet of the narrative paradigm moves away from social-scientific reductionism in the study of the church. It moves toward what is called crucial exploration of the communal identity of congregations as it is lived and not lived in light of the biblical narrative in the ongoing common life and in worship, preaching, education, and arguing.[11] In this facet of the narrative paradigm, congregational life is seen by the seminary as a gift from God. Through their lives and observed and remembered narrations, congregations become *valued sources* in theological education for exploring critically the common character and life in which both clergy and congregation are called to participate. Congregations become important *contexts* within which seminarians practice ministry under the joint supervision of seminary and congregation. And, congregations become *participants* with the seminary in the processes of teaching/learning, leading/following, and faith action/reflection (praxis) that contribute to a faith story lived in common.

THE ROLE OF A VOCATIONAL NARRATIVE IN THEOLOGICAL EDUCATION

The tasks of the seminary, local congregation, and the denomination are linked together inextricably because of an overarching mission or purpose that takes on shape and meaning in narrative form. While each of the three has

Truth and Tradition

distinct functions unique to it, the overarching mission of all three is to participate in God's unfolding narrative of the establishment of God's rule and reign on earth, which is announced and described in Scripture. It is not always clear that the seminary, the local congregation, and the denomination articulate and act with one accord on this overarching mission. Much tension exists because of this discrepancy.

The challenge today for the seminary and the congregation is to become intentional partners in dialogue aimed toward bringing about a clearer articulation of the overarching mission. However, it is important for seminary and congregation to be in dialogue about common ways they can participate in the overarching mission. Central to this discussion is the meaning of vocation that follows the seminary's assessment of its mission.

Assessing the Mission of Theological Education

The mission of theological education has characteristically focused on three related audiences or publics. These have included the academy—or the scholarly community—the church, and the world at large. Those who talk about the mission of theological education usually do it in comprehensive ways that are inclusive of all three publics. These publics often exist in tension with one another. For example, tension results from the perception that the scholarly community relates its work dominantly to those within it rather than to the church. Tension also results from the perceived failure of theological scholarship to connect with the practical fields.[12]

Further tension develops between the publics addressed by the seminary when it is perceived that the seminary considers the dominant issues that confront society to the exclusion of other more potent concerns. As a case in point, in the 1950s and 1960s the civil rights movement

Congregation and Academy

was something that the seminary considered important to address. In the late 1960s and the 1970s the seminary addressed the issues of the Vietnam War and the issues of the Cold War between U.S. democracy and communistic nations. Currently, the concerns of ecology, nuclear proliferation, AIDS, homophobia, racism, sexism, ageism, violence, and abuse in families are among the many concerns of theological education. Depending on the urgency that is felt around these issues, the seminary curricula have attempted to assign priorities to these concerns. The priority of these issues and how they are addressed by seminaries have direct impact on how the seminary relates to its publics and formulates its purpose.

Historically, Protestant theological seminaries have been concerned with the training of leadership for the church. The dominant issues of society and the concerns of the scholarly community have figured prominently in how the seminary has carried out its purpose. Because the church has often been viewed as an embodiment of societal ills and problems, a key purpose of the seminary has been to educate seminarians to become change agents who are able to transform congregations. The resources of the scholarly community are drawn on to accomplish this primary task.

The denomination responds to the perceived need to educate seminarians to be change agents in local congregations by emphasizing that local congregations need to be viable and vibrant communities in ministry. Some denominational leaders view the emphasis on change agentry as potentially destructive to the life in the local congregation. They want theological curricula that they feel are more friendly to local congregations. In response, some seminary faculty feel that the denominational leadership is seeking to avoid its true role in transforming church and society. Consequently, an "either-or" split emerges in which the transformation of the church and society is viewed as inconsistent with developing viable local congregations.

Truth and Tradition

Toward a Common Vocation for Seminary and Congregation

An important means of resolving the destructive tension among the seminary, denomination, and congregation is the intentional focus of the seminary and its faculty on a sense of vocation that is common to all. *Vocation* connotes a sense of mission and purpose that transcends the particular and unique purpose of the congregation, seminary, and denomination.[13]

Vocation points to a larger life narrative in which each must participate. This vocational narrative concerns the purposes of God as revealed in Jesus' coming to announce that the rule and reign of God is at hand and has begun. In this narrative, seminary professors, seminarians, local congregations, and denominations envisage themselves as servants of God's rule and reign. They also articulate their task as that of making seminarians, ministers, and laity aware of their role as servants working to hasten God's rule and reign. They see themselves as mutually responsible for and in ongoing mutual dialogue on the fulfillment of this task.

Because the common vocation is focused on God's rule and reign to which a vocational narrative of servanthood responds, neither the seminary, the local congregation, nor the denomination is an end in itself. Rather, they all exist as vehicles for bringing about God's rule and reign on earth. In this view, the seminary does recognize that the several publics exist; however, the publics are not central. Rather, the presence of God in all of life, working to establish God's rule and reign on earth, is the center and starting point of the emphasis on a vocational narrative of servanthood. This starting point is the normative basis for the seminary/congregation partnership. To articulate this normative basis explicitly is to profess or affirm the overarching reason for the existence of seminary, congregation, and denomination. It also is a way of professing or affirming the commitments all have to fulfill the narrative of servanthood. Failing to articulate the presence of God explicitly as the basis of the partnership relegates it to the position of "a ghost" in a machine, and the result is confusion in purpose.

Vocational Emphasis as Movement from Defundamentalization to Theological Formation

An emphasis on a vocational narrative of servanthood, focused on God's rule and reign, challenges any emphasis in seminaries on defundamentalizing seminary students' thinking as means of transforming the church. That is, it counters the task of theological education as that of "shaking the foundation" of "theologically conservative" students to the end that they acquiesce to mandates of plural ways of being, thinking, and acting in the world. Rather, the task of the seminary is to be a context in which seminary faculty and seminarians enter into the kind of dialogical partnerships that are needed in congregations. These are partnerships that center on a vocational narrative of servanthood.

The partnership task is ultimately a task focused on theological formation of the seminarian, the ongoing theological formation of the faculty, and theological formation of congregations. Theological formation is a process of discernment, critical reflection, and self-disclosure centered on God's presence and activity in every area of life and on human response to God through a vocational narrative of servanthood.

In every segment of the curriculum, theological formation through dialogical partnerships requires faculty and seminarians to engage in discerning and reflecting critically upon God's presence and activity in their lives, in congregations and denomination, in society, and in the world. It requires that they draw on congregational life and academic disciplines in determining where the vocational narrative of servanthood is or is not found. Moreover, it requires that, together, they self-disclose insights gained and challenges raised from congregational life, the academic discipline being considered, and from partnership processes. In short, *theological formation requires dialogical partnerships in every discipline where discernment, critical reflection, and self-disclosure can occur regarding God's intent, presence, and activity in congregations.*

Focus on a vocational narrative in theological education requires consideration of the nature of God's call to people to live out the call as well as consideration of people's stories within which the call comes. This focus also requires consideration of how those called people see themselves connected to congregations; how they may cooperate with God's activity in congregations; and their relationship with congregations. These considerations are pivotal aspects of theological formation.

Theological formation requires that seminaries elicit responses to basic questions across the academic disciplines. These responses should assist seminarians in partnership with faculty and congregations to address the nature of the vocational narrative of servanthood and its connection to congregational life. These basic questions include: Who am I? To what am I called? What is my story? What are the stories of people in congregation, denomination, society, and the world? Where is God in those stories? How may I cooperate with God's active involvement in these stories out of faith, showing God's love in just and caring ways? In short, *theological formation requires opportunities, including those offered in congregations, to respond to the critical questions that underlie the vocational narrative and its embodiment in congregations.*[14]

Considering what it means to heed God's direction toward a specific role in the vocational narrative is an important aspect of theological formation. That is, the task of seminaries is to provide opportunities across the academic disciplines wherein seminarians consider various roles needed to carry out lives of faith, hope, and love, as well as specific roles to which they are called.

This task includes consideration of roles and functions that are aimed toward both transformation and conservation. In transforming ministries, roles and functions are aimed toward institutional changes in order that their stories reflect faith, hope, and love. In conserving ministries, roles and functions are aimed toward maintaining institutions while their structures and activities are transformed in service of stories of faith, hope, and love. In this model of vocation, then, change and transformation are not ignored.

Accomplishing the role-oriented task requires that the nature of roles and functions of a called people become part of the deliberations in the disciplinary areas. It also requires that seminaries forge creative partnerships with organizations in diverse communities external to the seminary wherein a variety of roles and functions may be observed, examined, and undertaken. In this regard, partnership with congregations and denomination is seen as essential. In short, *theological formation requires opportunities to consider the nature of ministries of transformation and conservation and to consider and practice roles and functions, including those within congregations, that are needed in ministries in diverse communities.*

FORMING A COMMON ECCLESIOLOGICAL LANGUAGE

It is important to note that the seminary, the congregation, and the denomination hold the vocational narrative in common. All are called to help people live out the

Truth and Tradition

vocational narrative, whereby God's reign of redemptive love is communicated. However, the role of the seminary in giving shape to this emphasis is unique. It is unique because the seminary exists as a special context for the theological formation of people called by God, not because they are less sinful or more holy but in order to fulfill particular functions within the life and mission of the church in the world.[15] As a special context, the seminary is rightly understood as a representative form of the church. When the seminary is fully identified as a representative form of the church, it can be envisaged in covenant relationship with congregations and denomination, who themselves are representative forms of the church.

The identity of the church represented by the seminary, congregation, and denomination is that of an explicit Christian community where Christian commitment is nurtured and affirmed. In addition, these three institutions share the same overarching narrative, which gives shape to everything that is done within them. In sharing this overarching narrative, they exemplify the Body of Christ, which in its many forms, blends together to the glory of God and the service of humankind.[16] This understanding is the starting point for a common ecclesiological language on which intentional partnership between seminary and congregation can be based.

Historically, the language the church has used to communicate within itself and to the world has been largely narrative in form. Moreover, the narrative nature of congregational life is documented in the work of Hopewell. His work revealed that the congregation's self-perception is communicated primarily through narrative. Congregational members communicate among themselves primarily by story. Through their congregating, congregations participate in narrative structures of the church and world societies.[17] Likewise, the work of seminaries and the life within them are carried out and communicated to others external to them in narrative form. Seminaries also participate in the narrative structures of the church—local and global—and of the world's societies. Narrative is the common language that can enable seminary and congregation to be in partnership.

The Nature of Narrative as Common Language

Human beings and human institutions fundamentally develop ongoing narratives about their common life together. Individuals have personal narratives; marriages have conjugal narratives; families have family narratives; local congregations have their congregational narratives; denominations have their denominational narratives; and, seminaries have their seminary narratives. Each organism, whether individual or corporate, lives out its narrative and finds ways to celebrate it. In this way it keeps the narrative alive and vital. Narratives become the articulated stories that govern the lives of each organism whether for good or ill. No person or institution can survive without a narrative.

Narrative is a language of plot. It follows the logic of plots rather than linear logic. Plot logic sees narratives unfold. Plot logic focuses on the shifts in directions of the unfolding narratives as well as interruptions and destructive elements that enter into the narrative. Moreover, the language of narrative orients all other narratives to an overarching central narrative. This overarching central narrative forms the common mission for the seminary, local congregation, and denomination. This common narrative relates to the story of God establishing God's reign on earth as revealed in Scripture. The overarching story gives each of these entities a living plot and a narrative logic for their common mission.

The overarching plot is an eschatological plot. Despite all of the shifts in direction and disruption of God's intent, the plot is moving toward a purposeful end. This purposeful end is the eventual establishment of God's rule and reign on earth. As seminary, congregation, and denomination participate in their common mission, they also are participating in God's unfolding narrative. As partners, all move toward a common goal even though unique roles exist for each of them. It is the eschatological plot that gives each unique role its ultimate end.

THE SEMINARY AND CHURCH IN PARTNERSHIP

Partnership means that the seminary and local congregations see their roles as complementary and their work together as mutual. Partnership becomes concrete as seminary and congregations engage in ongoing dialogue. The seminary can promote this kind of partnership by seeking from congregations the answer to the question, How may we serve you? In this way, the seminary becomes a servant leader, understanding its role not in terms of status but rather in terms of bridge-building service. Its function is focusing on and relating to people in the midst of scholarly ideas.[18] Such a partnership creates supportive relationships and mutual respect between the seminary and congregations. And, the way that the seminary relates to the congregations helps the seminary to fulfill its servant mission.

Structures are needed to carry out partnerships between seminary and congregations. Structures refer to relational patterns through which seminaries can enter into dialogue with congregations. There are at least four kinds of relational patterns. Three of the four kinds of relational patterns are most commonly used by seminaries. One pattern is the *faculty/congregation relationship*. Through this pattern, seminary faculty themselves participate in and contribute to local congregational life. They fulfill various and somewhat different roles in the seminary classroom and in the congregation, but the essence of their involvement is quite interconnected. For them, participation in and contribution to congregational life as well as in classroom and community-wide activities of the seminary are infused with the same spiritual reality. Moreover, their understanding of the self's connection with congregational life makes it possible for them to draw insights from congregational life in the seminary classroom.

A second pattern by which seminaries commonly connect with local congregations may be termed the *seminary class/congregation relational pattern*. Typically, in this pattern, seminary faculty connect classes with local congregations by taking them into the congregational context or by inviting pastors and members of congregations into the classroom to "tell the stories" of who they perceive themselves to be, as well as their needs, challenges, triumphs, hopes, and ministry initiatives. By doing this, seminary faculty seek to make class material relevant as well as to foster critical thinking by infusing the academic discipline they teach with a contemporary "people" perspective.

The third most commonly used pattern is the *institutional/congregation relationship*. Through this structure, seminary students are connected to congregations through the seminary's field education program. Local congregations function as supervised practicum sites for seminarians.

A fourth relational pattern, not commonly used, may be referred to as *denominational forums for seminary/congregation dialogue*. In this pattern, the denomination promotes dialogue between seminaries and local congregations by initiating systematic scheduling as well as contexts for seminaries and congregational representatives to come together. The Association of Theological Schools' Quality and Accreditation Project during

1993 and 1994 was an important forum in which leaders in theological education could address the question, What is the "good" theological school?[19] It would further the cause of connecting seminary with congregation to engage in periodic forums in which seminary and representatives from diverse congregations focused on the questions: What stories do we hold in common? What is the partnership we need? Are there patterns of partnership that deserve attention?

The challenge in theological education today is to envision how structures for relating the seminary to congregation can be formed and utilized in more intentional ways throughout the curriculum. Moreover, the challenge in theological education is to identify roles for congregations in relating seminary with congregation, roles that affirm the integrity of the congregation's claim on seminary activity as well as the seminary's academic integrity. Optimally, both challenges are addressed in the process of dialogue between seminary and congregations. Four potential roles might be considered. The first role is *the congregation as source*. In this relational role, the narratives of diverse congregations are brought into dialogue with course materials in the various disciplines. The second role is *the congregation as context*. In this role, the congregation within the community is the location of course activities. Use of this role in relating is not confined to field education and is intended to move beyond classroom-bound approaches to theological education. The third role is *the congregation as leader/teacher*. In this role, pastors and members are utilized as co-leaders/co-teachers in course activities. Finally, a potential role is *the congregation as follower/learner*. In this role, pastors and members of congregations become beneficiaries of the expertise and publications written by seminary faculty and of guidance and information given by seminarians.

They also become learners in seminary-sponsored educational forums.

SUMMARY

This chapter addressed the concern of how the seminary and congregation can be linked in accomplishing their common mission. While the church and seminary have unique tasks and purposes, they also have the common mission of participation in the establishment of God's rule and reign. The narrative paradigm was suggested as a model that both could use in their common endeavors as well as in their unique tasks. The seminary and congregation can mutually enrich each other while they work together in their common mission. There is no need for them to be alienated from each other as they accomplish their unique tasks and their common mission.

NOTES

1. See Joseph C. Hough, Jr., and Barbara G. Wheeler, *Beyond Clericalism: The Congregation as a Focus for Theological Education* (Atlanta: Scholars Press, 1988); Joseph C. Hough, Jr., "The Education of Practical Theologians," *Theological Education* (Spring 1984): 55-84; Bruce W. Jackson, "Urban Theological Education for Church Leadership," *Urban Mission* (December 1993): 32-43; Gregory P. Rogers, "What Is Needed in Theological Education," *The Journal of Pastoral Care* (Spring 1992), 53-63; and Glenda Hope, "Revisioning Seminary as Ministry-Centered," *The Christian Century* (February 1-8, 1989), 107-11.
2. Darryl G. Hart, "The Troubled Soul of the Academy: American Learning and the Problem of Religious Studies," *Religion in American Culture* (Bloomington: Indiana University Press Center for the Study of Religion and American Culture, 1992), 66.
3. Ibid.
4. Ibid.
5. Hough, "Education of Practical Theologians," 64.
6. See also David H. Kelsey and Barbara G. Wheeler, "The ATS Basic Issues Research Project: Thinking About Theological Education" 30:2 (Spring 1994): 77-78.
7. Hough, "Education of Practical Theologians," 64-65.

Truth and Tradition

8. See James F. Hopewell, "A Congregation as a Focus for Theological Education," in *Beyond Clericalism: The Congregation as a Focus of Theological Education*, ed. Joseph C. Hough, Jr., and Barbara A. Wheeler (Atlanta: Scholars Press, 1988), 1-9.
9. See John B. Cobb, Jr., "Ministry to the World: A New Professional Paradigm," in Hough and Wheeler, eds., *Beyond Clericalism*, 24.
10. See Allan J. McNicol, "Skills, Credentials, or Faithfulness? Reflecting on Theological Education," *Christian Studies* (Austin: Institute for Christian Studies, 1992), 19-28.
11. David H. Kelsey, "A Theological Curriculum About and Against the Church," in Hough and Wheeler, eds., *Beyond Clericalism*, 40-43.
12. See Philip S. Keane and Melanie A. May, "What Is the Character of Teaching, Learning, and the Scholarly Task in the Good Theological School?" in *Theological Education: The Good Theological School* 30:2 (Spring 1994): 39.
13. See Melinda R. Heppe, "Finding a Shared Theology: The Common Tradition May Be Returning," *In Trust* (Spring 1994), 11.
14. Hough identifies faith, hope, and love as virtues that identify the Christian community. See Joseph C. Hough, Jr., "The Education of Practical Theologians," 59-61.
15. See Donald E. Messer, *Contemporary Images of Christian Ministry* (Nashville: Abingdon Press, 1989), 64.
16. Joseph C. Hough, "The Education of Practical Theologians," 58.
17. James Hopewell, *Congregation: Stories and Structures*, ed. by Barbara G. Wheeler (Philadelphia: Fortress Press, 1987), 46.
18. See Bruce Jackson, "Urban Theological Education," *Urban Mission* (December 1993): 41-42; Donald Messer, *Contemporary Images of Christian Ministry* (Nashville: Abingdon, 1989), 106-15; and Martin Marty, "The New Church and the Seminaries," *Dialog* 26:124-127 (Spring 1987): 125.
19. See James L. Waits, exec. ed., *Theological Education* 30:2 (Spring 1994).

Chapter Six

Immigrants and Pioneers

Neal F. Fisher

The conversation in this book began with a look at the current context for discussing theological education. In subsequent chapters we turned our attention to a series of topics with clear bearing on the future of theological education. This concluding chapter outlines some of the themes that rightfully claim a place in theological education for the years ahead. This discussion does not attempt to project the exact shape that seminaries will take in the next twenty years but to look at what is basic in theological education and to outline those elements for the future that grow out of the fundamental nature of theological education itself.

There are those who believe that the days of the seminaries themselves are numbered. Some believe, for example, that future pastors and other church leaders will come from the megachurches (those of two thousand members or more) and will receive their most effective training in that context. They understand the megachurches to be the best candidates to replace the "farm clubs" of earlier years—that is, the youth organizations, church schools, and successful congregations, which in former years challenged youth to consider ordained ministry and guided them to denominational seminaries.[1] Some believe that theological education will be decentralized, taking place

Truth and Tradition

in large congregations supplemented by leadership from other centers via interactive TV, satellite disks, and other means of electronic communication.[2]

No doubt the seminaries that are effective contributors to the church in the century ahead will undergo significant organizational and institutional changes. Without question the availability of interactive TV, computer networks, satellite hookups, and a host of other innovations, which we can now barely imagine, will materially influence the shape of seminary curricula, the qualifications of the professors, the method and location of teaching, the composition of the libraries, the schedule of classes, the living situations of the students, and virtually everything about the seminary.

We here want to approach the question at a more basic level, questioning what aim should inform theological education and what basic approaches should be considered for effectively accomplishing that aim. Our observation is that most of the discussions about whether seminaries are needed in the future or whether they will be replaced by megachurches or electronic communications beg important questions concerning the aim of theological education. These discussions assume—but do not articulate—at the outset a certain view of theological education and what it should accomplish. The implicit assumption often appears to be that theological education should aim to convey information (how to interpret the Bible, how to understand theological concepts, and others) or to train in techniques (how to organize a singles' ministry, how to lead a group discussion, how to organize a worship service, and more). The work of seminaries certainly includes these activities, but we hope to address the core and unity that underlies these and many other efforts of the seminaries.

A Changed Situation

We cannot think meaningfully about the future of United Methodist theological education without reminding ourselves at the outset of the new situation we face in the seminary, the church, and in the wider society.

A Changed Student Constituency

Discussion in chapter 3 noted that whereas in former years ministerial candidates with a vital experience of God's grace in their lives came to the seminary to illuminate this experience through further study of scripture, rhetoric, and theology; now the men and women who are responding to a call into ministry often have little structured experience in the church. Frequently they come to the seminary to search out the meaning of their call and to construct a personal faith that will integrate their lives. More often now than in the past students understand themselves as seekers rather than adherents. In some instances the goal of their quest appears to be more closely related to their individual identity than "the internalization of a communal religious tradition which is the condition for fruitful spiritual self-expression."[3]

Many of today's seminarians have had little experience in church school or organized youth groups, summer institutes, and other such programs that helped to guide the spiritual formation of earlier generations. Their college or university education, even if it has taken place on the campus of an institution affiliated with a church, will likely not have prepared them for seminary in the manner in which their predecessors were prepared. Often, even on the campus of church colleges and universities, subject matter is taught with a mind-set that effectively brackets religion and religious thought from any role save that of a private disposition or subjective inclination. Naturalistic and materialistic worldviews frequently prevail, even on the campuses of church-related institutions. The campus religious programs instituted by the churches to counterbalance this trend throughout the century are themselves finding it difficult to reach any significant portion of the campus population.[4]

This characterization is not intended to apply to all students; nor is it intended in any way to demean those students who match the description. It is simply to recognize that men and women coming to seminary today, persons who are attempting to hear and heed God's call, are coming out of a background and an intellectual mindset that contrasts markedly with the background of those who earlier enrolled in theological seminaries. Furthermore, as pastors and educators they are facing a culture that at least by some measures is more secular than the one confronted by their predecessors. The task of interpreting the world through the perspective of faith and leading a community of faith in embodying their faith in the present context surely will call for even more spiritual and theological acuity and vision in the years ahead than in the past.

The mission of the seminary for the years ahead, we hold, has been enlarged from that of equipping a person already confirmed and formed in the faith for ministerial leadership. The task now at hand for theological education is helping men and women who have responded to the call of God into ministry to be formed in the faith and in some cases to undergo a kind of conversion in preparation for their ministerial service. This expansion of the mission of the seminary is a tacit recognition that formation as a Christian leader requires an appropriation of a view of the world and a "plausibility system" at some variance with some of the dominant views found in society in general. The seminary, as we shall see, may come to bear a closer resemblance to ancient academies for the "schooling of the soul" than they do to the research universities.

A New World

If the individuals who enroll in the seminaries often come from distinctively different backgrounds than their predecessors a generation ago, the world in which they will serve is radically changed as well. By that we mean more than the obvious changes taking place, such as the dissolution of the Soviet Union and the accelerating pace of change in electronic communications, computing, and other inventions of technology. Underlying these momentous changes are alterations in the way we interpret our world.

Prevailing models by which we construe and understand the world (our paradigms and plausibility systems) are regularly replaced, and a profusion of competing and sometimes mutually exclusive models are employed simultaneously. Writers such as Thomas Kuhn, Michael Polanyi, and others have reminded us that the schools of interpretation (such as "the scientific worldview") by which we interpret the world are themselves historical traditions whose basic tenets are embraced more as a commitment than as an irrefutable scientific conclusion.[5]

We alluded earlier in this discussion to the ambiguity singled out by Vaclav Havel, President of the Czech Republic. He suggested that we are not of one mind in our view of science and religion. "By day," he said, "we work with statistics; in the evening we consult astrologers."[6] The new situation to which Havel alludes is one that is referred to frequently as "postmodern." This term has no uniformly honored meaning, but it is an indication that the world to many has a different feel. People experience "a rising sentiment of disaffinity," to use Albert Bormann's felicitous phrase, "a growing feeling that the kinship with what had gone before was being attenuated and lost."[7] What this experience portends, says Bormann along with many others, is a major transition in Western history.

The period of the Enlightenment was launched with the promise that universal reason would provide a unifying force for a humanity then (and now) so tragically rent by religious wars. No one is seriously contending that the scientific rationality that has been so dazzling in its success—even if representing a decidedly mixed presence for humanity and the environment on which humanity depends—is quickly to disappear. There is mounting evidence, however, of decidedly second thoughts on the scientific worldview spawned by scientific rationality and substantial doubts about—or outright repudiation of—some of its most orthodox doctrines.

For example, we have been taught that the manner in which we arrive at the truth of an entity is to divide it into its constituent elements and to weigh and measure them objectively. The route to the truth lies in objectification, separating ourselves from the object. Having been so successful by these objective means, some have taken the next step to say that only that which can be weighed and measured is real. All other statements reveal something, perhaps, about our subjective states, but they provide no reliable evidence whatsoever about a real state of affairs beyond.

However much these truisms of the Enlightenment guide us in certain laboratory procedures, as general outlooks and perspectives on life they are dated and discredited. For one thing, if there is anything we moderns have learned, it is that we understand elements of experience not in their isolation but in their relationship. To isolate and dissect will doubtless help us gain some insight into the makeup of an object, but we will not have comprehended what is most important for us to know about it until we have related it to a larger field.[8]

Immigrants and Pioneers

The dispute about knowledge was not, of course, the only shift introduced by the Enlightenment. That massive movement so prevalent for more than three centuries shifted explicitly from God as the center to the human subject as the center of the world. It focused upon the individual or the emancipated self, an emphasis still evident in Western culture. It rested hope in the progress thought to come by abolishing superstitution and by increasing knowledge.[9]

Now our situation is changed markedly. Many believe that we are witnessing today a rebirth of faith and the disintegration of Enlightenment thinking. For example: (1) The orthodoxy for many in the past held that the idea of God was superfluous and rapidly disappearing from human experience. Now a new conversation about God appears to be coming from the ranks of cosmologists and physicists, as well as from many others in less specialized pursuits. (2) It has not been so easy, as we were promised, to find in secular thinking a firm basis for morality. Values and ethics appeal implicitly to a comprehensive vision of the "way things are" or a larger narrative of human life. (3) The secularized eschatology in the form of belief in progress has crashed hard on the reality of evil. (4) Knowledge, promised to be inherently good, has been shown to be capable of both elevating and brutalizing humankind. (5) Emphasis upon the individual, significant as it is for human rights and freedoms, is by itself inadequate to understand the interrelationships of people with one another and with the environment around them.[10]

It appears now that there is an opening for religious faith in a world which had supposedly outgrown it. When people around the world, told for decades that religious faith was an illusion—or worse—still seek religious depth, the words of Simone Weil sound more prophetic than ever: "The danger is not lest the soul should doubt whether

Truth and Tradition

there is any bread, but lest, by a lie, it should persuade itself that it is not hungry."[11]

It is not yet apparent whether the undermining of the Enlightenment mind-set will eventuate in a more ready recognition of the deep hunger within or in a more cynical, relativistic stance toward human knowing. Whatever the outcome, it is clear that our world in the years ahead is decidedly changed. Paul held that when we are converted to a different perspective, we live in a different world. "When anyone is united to Christ," he wrote to the Corinthians, "there is a new world; the old order has gone, and a new order has already begun" (2 Corinthians 5:17 NEB). There is every indication that we are at one of those seams of history in which our worlds are changing. New worlds are coming into being, and old worlds are coming apart.

In such an intersection, it is natural that there be many shifts and turbulence. Strikingly, some denominations, such as The United Methodist Church, which (to its credit) has attempted to interpret the Christian message in terms comprehensible to contemporary men and women, are losing the allegiance of many. Other denominations that have not engaged in such an effort find their ranks increasing. Some within the United Methodist community call upon us to restore the "ancient landmarks" to give us identity and bearing. Others adopt "new age" religions or otherwise drop out of church participation.

The point is that those who are to study at the theological seminaries in the coming years are going to serve most of their lifetimes in a world that is radically new. The sociologist Margaret Mead, reflecting upon the upheaval following World War II and the changes wrought by that tragedy, said that those who grew up before the war were now living in a world they had never known. "All of us who grew up before World War II are pioneers, immigrants in time who have left behind our familiar worlds to live

Immigrants and Pioneers

in a new age under conditions that are different from any we have known."[12]

In a real sense, those who are to study theology in the years ahead similarly are immigrants and pioneers, seeking to proclaim the faith in a world in which neither they nor we have ever lived. What sort of theological education will help them to proclaim the faith effectively in this new world?

INCLUSIVE IMAGES OF THEOLOGICAL EDUCATION

If we are to talk about the shape of theological education that will prepare a new generation of leaders in a world undergoing basic change, we need some inclusive model or picture of the role theological education is going to play in their preparation. One recent effort to clarify the aim and form of theological education by such images has been made by David Kelsey.

Kelsey proposes the Athenian and the Berlin models as symbols for two decidedly divergent approaches to theological education.[13] Neither of these organizing images or typologies is on its own adequate to subsume all theological education under itself, but each focuses upon a cluster of qualities that effectively characterize and call to mind an approach to theological education.

The Athenian Model

The Athens model of theological education refers to the pattern of character formation adopted by the early Christians from the Greeks, who had developed this form of character formation over a period of four centuries. The Greeks called it *paideia,* a form of character formation, and many early Christians came to think of their faith itself as a new kind of paideia and wrote in these terms as early as the first century. They spoke of the gospel as paideia given by God in Christ and the scriptures, focusing upon a conversion of the soul, and given power by the Holy Spirit.[14] For the Greeks, paideia aimed at schooling or "culturing" the soul. In general, it was marked by four qualities: (1) The aim of paideia was more than the accumulation of virtues; it was knowledge of the Good itself. (2) The Good was not only the basis of virtue, but it was divine. Paideia thus was both moral and religious formation. (3) Knowledge of the Good could not be taught directly; academic studies taught the Good indirectly and were intended to help the student arrive at the moment of insight when the Good was disclosed and known directly. (4) Knowledge of the Good required a conversion, a turning away from the focus upon the world of appearance and toward attention to the real, the Good.[15] This ancient pattern of character formation and learning can be traced through early Christian history, and it continued into the Middle Ages.

The Berlin Model

The Berlin model, by contrast, is a much more recent—even if now more prevalent—model of theological education. It is identified with the formation of the University of Berlin in 1810 and stresses research and professional education. The research model aims to help the student become proficient in the methods of research and thus to master the truth to be known about any subject studied. Whereas paideia stressed the authority of the tradition that was studied, the Berlin model employed methods to test rigorously any truth claims that were made and to build theories about the subject to be studied. If paideia is aimed at helping the student cultivate capacities to know God, the Berlin model aims at developing aptitude in doing research.

In practice theology was formed around three areas of study: Christian texts (the Bible) and Christian practices and teachings (matters to be researched historically); theology (matters to be analyzed philosophically); and practical theology (studies delineating the normative rules by which the Christian faith could be practiced).[16] In the nature of the case, education in the Berlin model is inherently less communal than the Athenian model. Its focus is upon the skilled researcher and the learners who gather around her or him seeking themselves to gain proficiency in conducting research. Its aim is not in the first instance the conversion of life but the acquisition of objectified knowledge and the formation of theory.

These two models are typologies. Neither one by itself is an adequate model of theological education, but together they do help us to evaluate these contrasting approaches and to see more clearly what is at stake in setting the goals of theological education and fashioning the methods by which those goals may be achieved.

ELEMENTS IN FUTURE THEOLOGICAL EDUCATION

It is clear that there are valuable elements in both of the models outlined above, and either one of the models can flourish only by borrowing liberally from the strengths of the other. It does appear to the writer, however, that some of the deficiencies now experienced in some aspects of theological education (e.g., the frequent division between critical theory and practice, the inadequate connection between scholarship and religious devotion, the rift between congregations and the seminary, etc.) seem highly unlikely to be solved within the confines of the Berlin model alone. Some adaptation and embrace of the more ancient Athenian model seems necessary if the benefits of the Berlin model are to be realized for the church of the

Truth and Tradition

future. We shall look in the following paragraphs at the shape such a model would take in the years ahead.

The Aim of Theological Education

For us, as for those who employed this model in foregoing centuries, the implicit assumption is that the purpose of theological education is to know God and to prepare to help others know God through leadership in and through the church.[17] Self-evident as that may seem, such an aim has not necessarily been the focus for the seminaries in much of our history. Frequently we have tended to assume that first-order theology (addressing God directly in prayer and praise) was in place before one entered seminary and that the student in seminary learned a body of theory (second-order theology) which could later be applied in her or his role as a pastor, teacher, or other church leader.

In the Athenian model, the aim of understanding God is placed in a central position. It is acknowledged, of course, that God, the Source, Limits, and Destiny of all that is, is not a subject taught in the manner employed in teaching U.S. history, or physics, or nineteenth-century English literature. Rather, the student is introduced into a community, and in that community finds a context for discovering the realities of Christian faith, including a relationship with and an understanding of God. Several practices and disciplines are found to help a person know God truly. The Athenian model, which we are commending, stands in some contrast to those images of theological education as instruction in certain practices or education in certain theories later to be applied. This model includes intellectual discipline, practical application, and spiritual insight, which together, it is hoped, form a context in which the student may come to understand God. Here "understanding" is saving knowledge or direct encounter and not merely information about God.

Ingredients in Theological Education

In ancient Greek and early Christian practice, there were three elements that constituted theological education: *praxis, theoria,* and *poiesis*. We have translated and adapted these categories into three compatible and parallel categories for the following discussion: reflective practice, critical theory, and spiritual formation.[18]

Reflective Practice. Our forebears who argued for the practical training of a preacher on the preaching circuit had some insights very much worth heeding today. Though they believed the preacher should study six hours every day, they also knew that there were learnings to be gained by direct engagement that were not available in any other way. These learnings, furthermore, represented not merely an *application* of a truth known through other means but a distinctive way of knowing.

In practice, a professional learns how to construe a situation, to assess the context, and learn which acts are fitting or not fitting in that situation. Donald A. Schoen has gained a great deal of support for his concept of the "reflective practitioner" in fields as diverse as engineering, medicine, and city planning. The term refers to the professional who is constantly interrelating practical experience with critical reflection on that experience. Schoen notes, for example, that 80 percent or 85 percent of the cases presented to a physician fail to fit into the standard categories for diagnosis and treatment and that she or he must constantly search for ways to comprehend and treat these "irregular" situations.[19]

In suggesting reflective practice as a basic category of theological education for the future, there are different levels of implication that we have in mind.

First, it means that actual experience in ministry is a worthy contributor to one's entire theological education and not just an experimental area in which to test out

Truth and Tradition

theories about practice gained through other means. Some pastoral skills, of course, can be learned finally only when they are practiced. The theoretical understanding of preaching a sermon, visiting the dying, organizing youth, or leading a prayer service matters for little unless the person actually is capable of functioning in that leadership role. Stated in other terms, the theological student has not really understood the theoretical background of these and other ministerial acts until she or he has effectively taken part in such leadership.

A second element involved in this stress upon practice is a corresponding emphasis upon the congregation. Here we mean not merely the *place* but the *perspective* of theological education. Obviously some theological education will take place on the "field," that is, in the church or in a place of public ministry. Some, such as John Cobb and Joseph Hough have made rather elaborate proposals for theological education that centers significantly in the congregation.[20] Several more modest proposals by both seminaries and churches have provided for more intentional use of the first few years of ministerial service following seminary. In that probationary period the seminary and the church might cooperate in reflective participation in ministry, particularly in those spheres of professional ministry that are taught more effectively in that context than in the classroom.[21] The widespread practice of an intern year is also a helpful step in this direction.

Without in any way limiting the value of these options, stress is here placed upon practice as a perspective in which all theological education should take place. If Christian faith is transmitted to and by a community in history, then we may assume that the significance of that faith and practice will be known effectively only in the context of the community that has accepted that faith as its norm. Kelsey refers to the congregational orientation as the *lenses* through which we view all of theological education.[22] Here the concept of practice is expanded beyond the individual and embraces the life of a community in history. Questions arising out of the worship and witness of the congregation form basic points of entrance into the study of scriptures, history, theology, preaching, education, and other subjects. Here the aim of theological education is not in the first instance to abstract certain theories from the fields of study. It may, in fact, require that the lines between fields of study themselves erode in order to bring the full insights of scripture, theology, the social sciences, and other relevant perspectives upon the concrete questions facing the congregation.

The notion of practice should be expanded even further as a part of theological education. The practice of the congregation is itself a vital element in reflecting critically upon doctrine. Latin American and Black liberation theologians have insisted that theology is the "second step," as Gustavo Gutierrez put it.[23] The first step is action in keeping with Christ's mandate to identify with the marginalized and dispossessed. Theology is critical reflection upon what we experience in that discipleship. We will not understand who Christ is and what God is doing in the midst of our history, say the liberation theologians, until we walk in that path. Practice precedes profession. Marianne Sawicki goes so far as to say that the vision of the risen Lord depends upon our experience of hunger, either our own or the alleviation of hunger in others. "For Luke," she says, "recognition of the Risen Lord is possible only within a community that knows both how to be hungry and how to feed the hungry."[24]

There is another relationship that should also be noted. Christian doctrines, to reverse the process, gain right to acceptance in significant measure by their capacity to keep the Christian community on the path of faithfulness. They show their aptness and cogency by the direction they

Truth and Tradition

give to faithful practice. A generation ago theologian John Baillie and others contended that the content of theological doctrines is measured in very practical terms closely related to practice. Theological doctrines are means of sustaining the practice of the Christian community, he held. Baillie puts it in the following terms: "No doctrine has right of place within our Christian theology unless we can show that the denial of it would disturb or distort the pattern of our Christian sharing in that *koinonia* or *agape* which goes back to Pentecost."[25]

Critical Theory. This heading reflects a second element in the Christian formation of the soul, the ability to engage in critical thought as one reflects upon the Christian message. In virtually every era of the church's history, there are those who suggest or imply that transmittal of the Christian message from one generation to another is little more than delivering the verbal propositions, creeds, or confessions to a new generation. Some grow impatient with the seminaries because they do not assure that the heart of the message is transmitted and embedded in a new generation of theological students. The efficacy of the seminary is measured by some according to the success in this effort.

Literal transmittal of verbal propositions might be all that was needed if the aim were indoctrination of the students rather than their appropriation of the faith. We have held that the aim of theological education is knowing God. That is a form of knowledge that is not gained by uncritically receiving doctrinal statements of the past; it involves critical thought and theory. Thomas Langford helpfully distinguishes between doctrine and theology. The former, he contends, is the consensus of the church at any one time about the truth of the Christian faith. Theology, on the contrary, is "doctrine in the making." It involves a certain tentativeness, trial and error and experi-

126

> Not creeds, but "knowing God" (Stamm: But, can we know God in opposition to the creeds?)

mentation. "Doctrine produces exploratory theology, but exploration enriches its parent."[26]

The work of the Christian lay or ordained theologian is to appropriate Christian faith and find one's identity in that faith not merely as an expression of his or her particular tradition but as a reference to a true state of affairs. The conviction of that truth cannot be claimed unless one has an opportunity critically to examine the way in which the claims of faith relate to all we know through other means. Nothing is more practical to the Christian than his or her rock-bottom conviction that what is most profound in faith is also most true and enduring. This is not to deny that a prior commitment affects our reasoning, nor is it to overlook that theology is "faith seeking understanding" (Anselm). It is to hold that we owe ourselves and the church of which we are a part our most searching scrutiny of the faith we hold to be true.

Charles Wood has suggested three theoretical questions that might serve as the focal points for Christian theoretical reflection. Concerning any witness to Jesus Christ, we should ask: *(a)* Is it an authentic witness to Christian tradition? Is the witness rooted in the heritage of faith of which we are heirs? *(b)* Is the witness really true? How is belief in it to be supported? How does it relate to other truths of which I am convinced? *(c)* Is this witness given in a manner appropriate to its context? Is it "fittingly enacted"?[27]

Spiritual Formation. The note of spirituality as an aspect of theological education has not been prominent in Protestant seminaries until recent years. This is not to imply that it has been considered insignificant in the past. Seminaries in the main have assumed a vital evangelical experience as the irreplaceable foundation for a seminary education. Contemporary students, as we have seen, many times enroll in seminary from an impulse to respond to a call or to engage in further exploration. Not all those

Truth and Tradition

enrolling in a seminary have the clarity they hope later to achieve concerning the nature of that call and God's will for their lives. In the Berlin model seminaries tended to consider the matter of spirituality as a consideration to be cared for by one's involvement in the church and in one's personal spiritual development.

In recent years the seminaries have assumed greater responsibility for this aspect of theological education, as well as the realms of practice and theory. *Spirituality,* as we use the term, refers to the relationship of the person to God, to others, and to the created order. Someone has said that the opposite of *spiritual* is not *worldly;* the opposite of *spiritual* is *deadly.*

Virtually all the United Methodist seminaries have intensified their attention to the spiritual formation of students in recent years. Many have instituted on a voluntary or a required basis small prayer groups patterned after John Wesley's class meetings. In these groups students, faculty, and staff covenant together to meet weekly, to participate in public acts of worship, to engage in deeds of mercy, and to pray for one another. Seminaries have also given greater attention to prayer and spirituality in the courses offered. Some seminaries have provided spiritual companions or spiritual guides to work with each individual in growing in the spiritual life. This emphasis is likely to continue into the future as a strong and necessary element of theological education.

Context: Cosmopolis

Eunice Mathews, daughter of Dr. and Mrs. E. Stanley Jones, reports that when she was a child, her parents welcomed to their home in Silapur, India, a visitor from North America. The American woman, arriving at about dusk, was struck by the beauty of the sunset. She remarked: "What a wonderful sunset for such an out-of-the-way place." Bishop James K. Mathews added in commentary: "There are many out-of-the-way places made by God, who has a reckless abandon in scattering the beauties of sunsets and sunrises all around the world."[28]

An indispensable quality for any Christian leader in the world taking shape is alertness to and appreciation of the beauty God has placed in diverse places, cultures, and races throughout the earth. The appropriate context for Christian service anywhere on the planet is that of the worldwide parish. The earliest paideia aimed to cultivate those virtues that would aid the student to contribute to the city, the polis. The education of the soul essential for Christian leaders in the years ahead must take place in the context of *cosmopolis,* the urbanized culture that is worldwide in scope.

Diversity. The linguistics department of the university where I serve is capable of teaching virtually any language in the world and can locate native speakers within its metropolitan area for a majority of them. One high school nearby is said to include youth with twenty-eight different native languages. It is now a commonplace that there are more Muslims in the Chicago metropolitan area than there are Episcopalians. We know that this diverse world is tightly interrelated. The late physician and popular writer on science Lewis Thomas said that the world can best be grasped not as an organism but as a cell.[29]

In such a context it is increasingly difficult to represent Western male experience as the norm in comparison to which all other experiences are mere variations. In theological education, as elsewhere, voices hitherto seldom heard are now raised, not only demanding to be admitted into the discussion but seeking to alter the nature of the discussion itself. Different racial groups, feminists, womanists, economically and socially marginalized people from the "Two-Thirds World," people who have been exploited and abused—these and many more now insist that talk about God must be transformed in the light of the distinctive experience they have undergone.

We well know that our ancient temptation is to identify God with some segment of reality, perhaps of our own creation, and thereby to direct our devotion to an artifact and not to the Ultimate. In biblical terms, that is idolatry. In so doing, we fall under the reproof of the psalm:

> These things you have done and
> I have been silent;
> you thought that I was one
> just like yourself.
> But now I rebuke you, and lay the
> charge before you. (50:21 NRSV)

Transcendence. What is at stake theologically in the discussion on pluralism is whether God is to be God or a tribal deity, a deity employed to confirm and legitimate the insights, practices, and position of one culture or a subgroup within that culture. It is clear that any witness to God will take place in some culture. We are no more likely to know God outside any cultural context than we are to speak or write without employing a language. Theological education that is authentically cross-cultural can help make us aware of the provisional quality of our cultural insights and help us thereby to supplement them with expressions of Christian faith from other cultural perspectives. In this manner we may hope to gain a richer grasp of the truth of Christian faith and to recognize with the veteran missionary to India, Lesslie Newbigin:

> There can never be a culture-free gospel. Yet the gospel, which is from the beginning to the end embodied in culturally conditioned forms, calls into question all cultures, including the one in which it was originally embodied.[30]

Theological education suitable for preparing for service in cosmopolis will not need to teach the student to scorn his/her own culture and thus become a cultural orphan in the world community. Interaction with other cultures will help us all appreciate aspects of our culture as well as to sense its weaknesses. Above all, we may hope that it will communicate the provisional quality of any culture and the message of God who at the same time both transcends any culture and gives evidence of the divine presence within it.

Truth. Many who name themselves "postmoderns" cite the diversity of cultures and conclude therefrom that anything that is said—because of its origin in some cultural setting—is on that account incapable of representing any truth beyond that particular setting. Important theological voices indicate that the meaning of the faith is to be understood solely within its "cultural-linguistic system."[31]

If such expressions merely mean to call our attention to the reality that Christian faith is understood within a context or path of discipleship, there is every reason readily to agree. But in fact these cautions are often intended to discourage any interest in or mandate for witnessing to a faith to those not already in its cultural-linguistic system, and there is reason to resist this conclusion. Peter Berger has reminded us that the dual inheritance of Hebrew and Greek culture is monotheism and the principle of contradiction, the conviction that one entity cannot be both A and non-A.[32] Religious faith in the nature of the case makes claims not merely about the individual's subjectivity, or that of the culture to which he or she belongs. Religious faith also makes reference to a real state of affairs. Because that real state of affairs is known to us inevitably in some cultural perspective does not deliver us from the obligation to discern elements of truth in other

Truth and Tradition

cultures and in so doing to supplement and correct our own cultural perspectives.

We can abandon the Enlightenment promise that scientific reason would provide a timeless, transcendent perspective from which to view all phenomena. But we are not left with pure relativism as our only alternative. There is a critical capacity embedded in the history of a tradition, as MacIntyre has reminded us, that helps to vindicate the efficacy of a tradition and to refine and correct the tradition itself.[33]

There need be no contradiction between faith in Jesus Christ as Lord and our readiness to learn from persons of other cultures and religions. We may be confident that God has disclosed the divine presence (as well as sunsets) in many places throughout the earth. In our encounter with persons of other religions, we may expect to learn more deeply the truth of God disclosed in Christ. In the words of John B. Cobb, Jr.:

> If we trust Jesus Christ as our Lord and Savior, we have no reason to fear that truth from any source will undercut our faith. Indeed, we have every reason to believe that all truth, wisdom and reality cohere in him. The more fully we are transformed by the wisdom that is accessible to us, the further we move toward that fullness of truth to which Christ directs us.[34]

The context for theological education now and in the future is cosmopolis. This requires on the part of the student a lively and appreciative acquaintance with cultures other than his or her own. It mandates a sensitivity to the evils of poverty, to the systemic oppression of whole peoples, to forces of attitudinal and institutional racism, and to violence and sexism and the other evidences of the principalities and powers. It demands as well a corresponding commitment to struggle against them. Preeminently it permits confidence in the universal significance of God's reign and readiness for service and discipleship within the hope conferred by that promise.[35]

We began this discussion by acknowledging that people in United Methodist and predecessor denominations were wary of theological seminaries. We have attempted in these pages to outline areas in which the seminaries and the denomination genuinely need one another. Neither can fulfill its mission without the other. These concluding comments, have been intended to suggest some perspectives by which the seminaries can be most faithful in their responsibilities to equip a generation of pioneers and immigrants to serve as effective leaders in and through the church. We may be sure that God continues to work in and through our history to accomplish the divine purposes. Let us pray that both the seminaries and the church of which they are a part may be found worthy instruments toward that end.

NOTES

1. See Lyle E. Schaller, *21 Bridges to the 21st Century* (Nashville: Abingdon Press, 199), 121-31.
2. See, for example, Russell Chandler, *Racing Toward 2001: The Forces Shaping America's Religious Future* (Grand Rapids: Zondervan Publishing House, 1992), 210-11.
3. George Lindbeck, "Spiritual Formation and Theological Education," in *Theological Education*, 24 (Supplement I, 1988): 17.
4. George M. Marsden, *The Soul of the American University: From Protestant Establishment to Established Nonbelief* (New York: Oxford University Press, 1994), especially 429ff.
5. See, for example, Thomas S. Kuhn, *The Structure of Scientific Revolutions*, 2nd ed. (Chicago: University of Chicago Press, [1962] 1970) and Michael Polanyi, *Personal Knowledge: Towards a Post-Critical Philosophy* (Chicago: The University of Chicago Press, 1958).
6. From an address by Vaclav Havel in Philadelphia, July, 1994. Reported in Nicholas Wade, "Method and Madness," in *New York Times Magazine*, 14 August 1994, 18.
7. Albert Bormann, *Crossing the Postmodern Divide* (Chicago: University of Chicago Press, 1992), 20.

Truth and Tradition

8. See Toulmin's insistence upon the importance of the context in knowing in Stephen Toulmin, *Cosmopolis: The Hidden Agenda of Modernity* (New York: Free Press, 1990), 187.
9. See the outlines of this summary in Paul G. Hiebert, "Globalization as Evangelism," in *The Globalization of Theological Education*, eds. Alice Frazer Evans, Robert A. Evans, and David A. Roozen (Maryknoll: Orbis Books, 1993), 64f.
10. These conclusions are outlined by Diogenes Allen, *Christian Belief in a Postmodern World* (Louisville: Westminster/John Knox Press, 1989), 2-5.
11. Simone Weil, *Waiting for God*, 210, as quoted in Diogenes Allen, *Christian Belief in a Postmodern World*, 214.
12. Margaret Mead, *Culture and Commitment* (Garden City, N.Y.: Doubleday, 1970), 74.
13. David H. Kelsey, *Between Athens and Berlin: The Theological Education Debate* (Grand Rapids, Mich.: William B. Eerdmans, 1993), especially 1-27.
14. David H. Kelsey, *To Understand God Truly: What's Theological About a Theological School* (Louisville: Westminster/John Knox Press, 1992), 69.
15. Ibid., 9.
16. Ibid., 17.
17. This assumption is spelled out helpfully and clearly in Kelsey, *To Understand God Truly*. The following comments rely significantly upon Kelsey's discussion.
18. Max Stackhouse provides a helpful discussion of this threefold composition of paideia showing their interrelationship in his *Apologia: Contextualization, Globalization, and Mission in Theological Education* (Grand Rapids, Mich.: William B. Eerdmans, 1988), chapters 6, 7, and 8.
19. See Donald A. Schoen, *The Reflective Practitioner: How Professionals Think in Action* (New York: Basic Books, 1983), 48f.
20. See their *Christian Identity and Theological Education* (Chico, Calif.: Scholars Press, 1985). For extensive responses to various portions of their proposed model, see Don S. Browning, et al., eds., *The Education of the Practical Theologian: Responses to Joseph Hough and John Cobb's Christian Identity and Theological Education* (Atlanta: Scholars Press, 1989).
21. See Marjorie Hewitt Suchocki's suggestions in this regard in her "A Learned Ministry?" in *Quarterly Review*, 13:2 (Summer 1993): 3-17.
22. Kelsey, *To Understand God Truly*, 157, 163.
23. Gustavo Gutierrez, *A Theology of Liberation: History, Politics and Salvation*, trans. and ed. Sister Caridad Inda and John Eagleson (Maryknoll, N.Y.: Orbis Books, 1973), 11.
24. Marianne Sawicki, "Recognizing the Risen Lord," *Theology Today* XLIV: 4 (January 1988): 449.
25. John Baillie, *The Sense of the Presence of God* (New York: Charles Scribner's Sons, 1962), 153.
26. Thomas A. Langford, "Doctrinal Affirmation and Theological Exploration," in *Doctrine and Theology in The United Methodist Church*, ed. Thomas A. Langford (Nashville: Kingswood Books, 1991), 206.
27. Charles M. Wood, *Vision and Discernment: An Orientation in Theological Study* (Atlanta: Scholars Press, 1985), 39-40.
28. Recalled in Eunice and James K. Mathews, "Remembrances of Dr. and Mrs. E. Stanley Jones," in *Theology and Evangelism in the Wesleyan Heritage*, ed. James C. Logan (Nashville: Kingswood Books, 1994), 188.

Immigrants and Pioneers

29. Lewis Thomas, *The Lives of a Cell: Notes of a Biology Watcher* (New York: Bantam Books, 1974), 4.
30. Lesslie Newbigin, *Foolishness to the Greeks: The Gospel and Western Culture* (Grand Rapids: William B. Eerdmans, 1986), 4.
31. George A. Lindbeck, *The Nature of Doctrine: Religion and Theology in a Postliberal Age* (Philadelphia: Westminster Press, 1984). See also William C. Placher, *Unapologetic Theology: A Christian Voice in a Pluralistic Conversation* (Louisville: Westminster/John Knox Press, 1989).
32. Peter Berger, *A Far Glory: The Quest for Faith in an Age of Credulity* (New York: Free Press, 1992), 40.
33. Alasdair MacIntyre, *Whose Justice? Which Rationality?* (Notre Dame: University of Notre Dame Press, 1988), 7ff.
34. John B. Cobb, Jr., "Being a Transformationist in a Pluralistic World," in *Christian Century*, 111:23 (August 10-17, 1994): 749.
35. This summary based on a statement on globalism given in William E. Lesher, "Living the Faith under the Conditions of the Modern World," in *The Globalization of Theological Education*, ed. Alice Frazer Evans, Robert A. Evans, and David A. Roozen (Maryknoll, N.Y.: Orbis Books, 1993), 37.

Contributors

Neal F. Fisher. President and Professor of Theology and Society, Garrett-Evangelical Theological Seminary, Evanston, Illinois. Previous writings include *The Parables of Jesus: Glimpses of God's Reign* and *Context for Discovery*.

Roger W. Ireson. General Secretary of the General Board of Higher Education and Ministry, The United Methodist Church. Before coming to the board, Dr. Ireson was pastor of St. Timothy's United Methodist Church in Detroit.

Robert C. Neville. Dean and Professor of Theology, Religion, and Philosophy, Boston University School of Theology. Dean Neville is former President of American Academy of Religion. His most recent writings include *Behind the Masks of God, God the Creator,* and *Highroad around Modernism*.

Judith E. Smith. Associate General Secretary, General Board of Higher Education and Ministry. The Reverend Smith has served pastorates in Oregon and has written extensively in church publications.

Contributors

She is a member of the Advisory Board, Lilly Endowment Project: United Methodism and American Culture.

Lovett H. Weems, Jr. President of Saint Paul School of Theology, Kansas City, Missouri. Dr. Weems served as a local pastor for eighteen years and is now a clergy member of the Missouri West Annual Conference. His previous writings include *Church Leadership* and *John Wesley's Theology Today*.

Anne Streaty Wimberly. Associate Professor of Christian Education and Church Music at Interdenominational Theological Center, Atlanta, Georgia. Dr. Wimberly is author of *Soul Stories* and *Language of Hospitality*.

Edward P. Wimberly. Jarena Lee Professor of Pastoral Care and Counseling, Interdenominational Theological Center, Atlanta, Georgia. Recent writings include *Prayer in Pastoral Counseling, Using Scripture in Pastoral Counseling,* and *African-American Pastoral Care*.

Seminaries of The United Methodist Church

Boston University School of Theology, Boston, Massachusetts

Candler School of Theology, Emory University, Atlanta, Georgia

Drew University, The Theological School, Madison, New Jersey

Duke University, The Divinity School, Durham, North Carolina

Gammon Theological Seminary, Atlanta, Georgia

Garrett-Evangelical Theological Seminary, Evanston, Illinois

Iliff School of Theology, Denver, Colorado

Methodist Theological School in Ohio, Delaware, Ohio

Perkins School of Theology, Southern Methodist University, Dallas, Texas

Saint Paul School of Theology, Kansas City, Missouri

School of Theology at Claremont, Claremont, California

United Theological Seminary, Dayton, Ohio

Wesley Theological Seminary, Washington, DC

Index

Andover, 15
Anselm, 10, 127
apprenticeship, 16, 21, 22
Aquinas, Thomas *(Summa Contra Gentiles)*, 10, 57
Association and Theological Schools, 80
  Quality and Accreditation Project, 108
Association of United Methodist Theological Schools, 80, 89
Augustine, 10

Baillie, John, 126
Barth, Karl, 10
Berger, Peter, 24, 131
Biel, Gabriel, 10
bigotry, 51, 54, 57
The Book of Discipline, 59
Borein, Rev. Peter, 17
Bormann, Albert, 115, 116
Broadus, John, 15
Burns, James MacGregor, 59

Calvin, John, 10, 44
Cannon, Bishop William R., 65
Carter, Stephen, 25
Chopp, Rebecca, 33, 63
"Christmas Conference" (1784), 16, 60

church
  changes in, 23-33, 42-43
  freedom/accountability balance, 82-84, 91
  future of, 73
  language of, 104-6
  leadership, 13, 27, 59. *See also* ministry
  mega-, 111, 112
  mission of, 50-53
  Monophysite, 41, 44
  /seminary partnership, 106-9
  See also congregation
circuit riders, 15, 25, 75
  apprenticeship of, 16, 21, 22
  uneducated, 17, 18
clergy
  effectiveness, 22, 28, 64, 81
  paradigm, 95, 96
  statistics, 61
  training, 123-28
  uneducated, 16-17, 18, 22
  See also ministry
Cobb, John B., Jr., 31, 124, 132
colleges, 18
  liberal arts, 17, 19
Cone, James, 32
"Confessions of a Grieving Seminary Professor" (Oden), 42
congregation
  changing culture of, 78-79

139

Index

"clergy effectiveness" discussion in, 81
middle-class, 17, 18, 24-25, 47
narrative language of, 105-6
and seminary education
  alienation to, 93-96
  financial support of, 78, 85
  paradigm for, 95-96
  roles in, 108-9
  students, 85-86, 90-91
See also church
cosmopolis, 128-29, 131, 132
countermovements, 55-56
Counter-Reformation, 41
Course of Study, 16, 20, 22, 76, 77, 85
cultural-linguistic system, 131
culture
  changing, 24-25, 78-79
  cosmopolis, 128-29, 131, 132
  diversity of, 129-30
  and expression of Gospel, 39-40
  transcendence of, 130-31
  and truth, 131-33
See also society

"The Danger of an Unconverted Clergy" (Tennent), 14
Dempster, John, 19
denomination, 25
  decline of, 26-27
  distinctiveness of, 28-29
  identity of, 71
  loyalty to, 87
  narrative language of, 105-6
discipline, 27, 28, 30
doctrine
  fidelity to, 21, 27
  theological, 126
  vs. theology, 126-27

Ebeling, Gerhard, 10
education, theological
  agenda priorities, 54-58
  apprenticeship system, 16, 21, 22
  Athenian model, 31, 119-20, 122
  Berlin model, 31, 119, 120-21, 122, 128
  and congregations, 31, 97, 106-9
    alienation to, 93-96
    roles in, 108-9

curriculum, 10-11, 87-88, 99, 112, 123-28
debate over
  early, 18-23, 30-33, 76
  present, 23-29, 76, 93
future of, 73, 111-19, 121-33
history of, 14-21
mission of, 98-100, 114-15
need for, 14-21, 53
priorities of, 37
purpose of, 30, 38, 122-23
vocational narrative in, 97-103
See also Course of Study, seminaries
Enlightenment, 25-26, 46, 116, 117, 118, 132
environmental concerns, 53, 54
The Evangelical Association, 15, 19-20
experience
  Christian, 23, 29, 31
  theological, 40-41

faith, rebirth of, 117-18
Farley, Edward, 30
Fisher, Neal F., 89
Fletcher, John, 16
Fraser, James, 21

Gardner, John, 62
Garrett, Mrs. Eliza, 17, 19, 20
Garrett Biblical Institute, 19, 20
General Conference
  of 1784, 16, 60
  of 1816, 16
  of 1847, 20
  of 1856, 19, 20-21, 27
  of 1908, 82
  of 1952, 76
  of 1956, 65
  of 1992, 64, 76
Good News movement, 55-56
Goodwin, Thomas, 18-19
Grandy, Jerilee, 66, 69
Great Awakening, 14
Gutierrez, Gustavo, 32, 125

Harnack, Adolf, 45
Havel, Vaclav, 26, 115
Hedding, Bishop Elijah, 19
Henry, John, 10

140

Index

heresy, 20, 21, 43, 55
holiness, 46-49
homosexuality, 27, 55,
Hopewell, James, 95, 104
Hough, Joseph C., Jr., 31, 95, 124

integrity
  of ministry, 63-64
  spiritual, 29

Job, Bishop Rueben P., 59
Jones, Dr. and Mrs. E. Stanley, 128

Keck, Leander, 65
Kelsey, David, 30, 31, 88, 119, 125
King, Martin Luther, Jr., 10
Kuhn, Thomas, 115
Kung, Hans, 10

LaGree, R. Kevin, 65
Langford, Thomas, 126
language, ecclesiological, 104-6
  narrative, 96-103
leadership
  definition of, 59-60
  See also ministry
learning
  sophisticated, 46, 50
Lewis, C. S., 52
Lilly Enlistment Project, 68
The Living God (Oden), 43
Luther, Martin, 10, 44
Lynn, Dr. Robert W., 73

MacIntyre, Alasdair, 132
Marty, Martin, 24, 63
Mathews, Eunice, 128
Mathews, Bishop James K., 129
McCulloh, Gerald *(Ministerial Education in the American Methodist Movement)*, 82
Mead, Margaret, 18
middle class, 17, 18, 24-25, 47
mindset, 24, 25-29
  Enlightenment, 118
Ministerial Education Fund (MEF), 71, 72, 78, 85
Ministerial Education in the American Methodist Movement (McCulloh), 82

ministry
  calling to, 59
  conserving, 103
  enlistment in, 60-69
  integrity of, 63-64
  learned, 38
  practice of vs. doing of theology, 88
  skills in, 28, 89
  transforming, 103
  See also clergy
minorities, 24, 27, 41, 49, 55
misconduct, sexual, 27-28, 42
mission
  of church, 50-53
  common, 105-6, 109
  of theological education, 98-100, 114-15
Mitchell, Hinckley, 82
modernity, 25-26, 42-43, 45
Mott, John R., 59
Mud Flower Collective, 32-33

narrative, 96-97
  as common language, 104-6
  vocational, 97-103
Newbigin, Lesslie, 130
Newbury Biblical Institute, 19, 20
New England Biblical Institute, 19
Northwestern Christian Advocate, 20

Oden, Thomas C., 42-45, 55
Ogden, Schubert, 62, 82
O'Neill, Joseph P., 66, 69
Orr, Judith, 60
outreach, evangelical, 46, 50

paideia, 119-20, 129
Panikkar, Raimundo *(Unknown Christ of Hinduism)*, 57
Pierce, Bishop George F., 21
pluralism, 10, 24, 130
Polanyi, Michael, 115
practice, reflective, 123-25
Presbyterians, 14, 15
Protestantism, 28, 41, 44-45, 73

Rahner, Karl, 10

Index

reason, 40, 42
  scientific, 132
Reformation, 41, 47
relational patterns
  denominational forums for seminary/congregation dialogue, 107-8
  faculty/congregation, 107
  institutional/congregation, 107
  seminary class/congregation, 107
revolution, sexual, 27
Roman Catholicism, 41, 47
Ruether, Rosemary Radford, 32

Sawicki, Marianne, 125
Schoen, Donald A., 123
science, 26
scripture, 40, 41, 42
seminaries
  and congregation, 31, 97, 108-9
    alienation to, 93-96
    roles in, 108-9
  control of, 84-92
  curriculum, 10-11, 87-88, 99, 112, 123-28
  debate over
    early, 18-23, 30-33, 76
    present, 23-29, 76, 93
  faculty, 30-33, 82, 94, 95, 107
  freedom/accountability balance, 82-84, 91
  funding of, 11, 71-72, 85
  future of, 73, 111-19, 121-33
  history of, 14-21
  investing in, 84-92
  location of, 31-32, 70
  narrative language of, 105-6
  non–United Methodist, 29, 69-70
  ownership of, 77-82
  partnership with church, 106-9
  Protestant, 99, 127
  purpose of, 9, 88
  tuition, 70, 72, 78
  United Methodist, 11-12, 69-71, 128
    listing of, 136-37
  See also education, theological; students
servanthood, 100-102
Sherer, Bishop Ann B., 73
social justice, 47, 48, 49, 54

society, 115-19
  changing, 42
  middle-class, 24-25
  pluralistic, 10
  and seminary location, 31-32
  See also culture
spirituality, 127-28
students, 27-28, 56, 62
  changes in, 113-15
  and congregation, 85-86, 90-91
  second-career, 67, 79, 86
  statistics, 66-67
  tuition, 70, 72, 78
  younger, 68-69
Suchocki, Marjorie, 90
Summa Contra Gentiles (Aquinas), 57
Systematic Theology (Tillich), 57

Tennent, Gilbert ("The Danger of an Unconverted Clergy"), 14
Theological Education Commission, 80
theological formation, 101-3
theology
  areas of study, 121
  Black, 32, 125
  vs. doctrine, 126-27
  doing of vs. practice of ministry, 88
  feminist, 32-33, 129-30
  liberation, 32, 33, 41, 125
  narrative, 96-97
  and the poor, 32
  positions of, 70
  Third-World, 27
  of truth and tradition, 37-50
  Wesleyan, 37, 40-41, 46-50, 74-75
theory, critical, 126-27
Thiemann, Ronald F., 61
Thirty Years' War, 25
Thomas, Lewis, 129
Tillich, Paul *(Systematic Theology)*, 10, 52, 57
traditions, 56-58
  ancient, 37, 43-45
  changing, 42
  Christian, 41-42
  and evangelization, 48-49, 50
  Pentecostal, 41
  Protestant, 44-45

Index

of reason and faith, 10
risking, 49
teaching, 9
theology of, 37-50
Treese, Donald H., 63
truth, theology of, 37-50
Two Percent Fund. *See* Ministerial Education Fund

University Senate, 79-80
universities
  Berlin, 120
  Boston, 19, 82
  Northwestern, 19
  Oxford, 14, 46
  Princeton, 15
  Vanderbilt, 21
Unknown Christ of Hinduism (Panikkar), 57

vocation, 100-103

Weil, Simone, 117
Welch, Claude, 94
Wesley, John, 10, 16, 23, 44-45, 46, 74, 128
Wesleyan theology, 37
  quadrilateral, 40-41
  tradition, 46-50, 74-75
White, Bishop Dale, 64
women, 27, 41, 44, 129
  agendas of, 51, 54-55, 56-57
  in leadership, 49
  seminary statistics, 66
Wood, Charles, 127
World Methodist Council, 49
worldview, 115-19